Writers of Wales

CW00375027

Editors
MEIC STEPHENS   R. BRINLEY JONES

Sam Adams

ROLAND MATHIAS

University of Wales Press

Cardiff 1995

I

When in 1985 Roland Mathias suffered a stroke, it seemed that a line had been drawn under one of the most varied, prolific and influential careers among men of letters in contemporary Wales. He has been, not by turns but for much of his life at the same time, poet, short-story writer, critic, editor, scholar, historian, preacher, lecturer and educationalist, and has distinguished himself in all these roles, and more. He spent the significant stages of his young life, home, school and university, in England, but has championed the cause of Welsh culture and particularly Welsh writing in English. His family roots lie deep in Welsh Nonconformity; he is a committed Christian. The stroke that stopped the flow of his wide-ranging activity has made an unwelcome opportunity for taking stock of his contribution. The personal loss he has borne with a benign fortitude that is founded in his religious conviction. The loss to life and letters in Wales has been incalculable.

Roland Glyn Mathias was born on 4 September 1915 at Ffynnon Fawr, a farmhouse (which is now demolished) in Glyn Collwn, above Talybont-on-Usk, Breconshire, and beyond the reservoir that has since filled much of the valley. The farm was the home of his mother's parents, Joseph and Rachel Morgan. They had both come originally from Y Ffawyddog, near Llangattock, a few miles further down the Usk, which looks from its hillside across the river to Crickhowell, but their path to Ffynnon Fawr had not been straight. Rachel Prosser, as she then was, had been an elementary schoolteacher in Crickhowell and later in Todmorden, Lancashire, before she married Joseph Morgan, a mason by trade. Joseph joined a small family building enterprise in Cardiff, and their daughter Muriel, who was to be Roland Mathias's mother, was born there in Arran Street, off City Road, in 1891. Joseph Morgan was by all accounts a strong and vigorous young man, but in Cardiff his health declined and, to save himself, he was advised to leave. In 1895 the family moved to a farm called Tyle-Clydach overlooking the hamlet of Aber, now just below the Talybont reservoir, and ten years later the short distance to Ffynnon Fawr. They attended the hillside chapel at Aber, one of the earlier outposts of Dissent.

Muriel was a sensitive and intelligent child. She became the first pupil from the elementary school at Talybont to pass the entrance examination to the Girls' County School in Brecon, which in those days entailed boarding in the town during the school week. She did well, and in 1910 was one of the first two candidates from the school to gain the Central Welsh Board Higher Certificate. She returned to her old elementary school in Talybont as a pupil-teacher, with a view to following subsequently a teacher-training course at a college. Readers of D. H. Lawrence will be familiar with the pattern. Unlike Ursula Brangwyn, Muriel Morgan could not find a way of coping with unruly children: she left the school and went back to help her mother on the farm.

Evan Mathias, Roland's father, was one of nine children. He was born in 1889, in a humble cottage beside the road at Gât Bwlch-clawdd, Rhos Llangeler, Carmarthenshire, where his parents, David and

Mali, made their first home. They were both of local stock, but when Evan was six, David Mathias, a skilled carpenter, builder and wheelwright, took his family to a house in Victoria Street, Llanelli, and found work as a carpenter on the Stepney Estate at 30 shillings a week. Evan, a lad of parts, thrived in the elementary and won a place in the grammar school. Supported by his father and elder brothers, he went on to the University College in Cardiff and then to train for the ministry at Coleg Coffa in Brecon, a course of study that extended in all to six years and meant no small sacrifice on the part of his family. His first pastorate was at Edwardsville near Merthyr Tydfil, but he was called soon afterwards to Pontypool Road Congregational Church, New Inn. He had barely time to establish himself there before the First World War began.

During his training at Coleg Coffa, Evan Mathias, who was eloquent in Welsh and English, frequently preached at Aber chapel. He and Muriel Morgan may have first met at the chapel, or possibly during her school-days in Brecon. In any event, a relationship developed and they were married on 7 December 1914 at Benaiah Chapel, Talybont-on-Usk.

At the outbreak of hostilities in August 1914, Evan Mathias had immediately asked for and been granted leave of absence from his church in New Inn to become a chaplain in the army. He and his bride had a week together in December in London before he joined the Royal Army Chaplains' Department in Purfleet.

The promptness of Evan Mathias's response to the call to join the army reveals the strength of his faith and his conviction that to serve in this way accorded with God's will. What his new wife's feelings were at that time we cannot guess, but they subsequently became very different from his. In unpublished papers, Roland Mathias has written about the stubbornly held and opposing views of his mother and father over many issues of deep significance. They were fundamentally unalike and neither would bend towards the other. He was sociable and outgoing, eager to travel, at ease in the pulpit or on the public platform; she was essentially private, truly content only in her own home. He, a well-respected eisteddfodwr, had a securely Welsh cultural identity; she, like her father (who carried to his grave the impression that he had been cheated by a conspiracy of local Welsh-speaking farmers when he took up the tenancy of Tyle-Clydach), was inclined to be anti-Welsh. The most serious cause of division between them, however, was the war and the concept of a military that served both God and country, which she found totally unacceptable. She is described as sensitive, timid, shy and retiring, but to withstand the considerable force of his character, she clearly possessed boundless reserves of moral strength. He seemed to his children irritable, stern, even harsh, yet he held a great concern for them and how they made their way in the world and, in later life, was the more attentive listener to accounts of their experiences.

In 1915, the newly enlisted chaplain went with the Royal Welsh Fusiliers to the Dardanelles and his wife continued to live in her family home, where, in September, their first son was born. She remained in Ffynnon Fawr until Joseph Morgan died in 1916. Then she moved with her family to Aber Farm,

Talybont-on-Usk, which was kept by her younger brother Emlyn. It was at this farm that the writer's brother, Alun, was born in July 1919.

Quinsy cut short Evan Mathias's service in the Dardanelles. He was shipped home and, when he recovered, he was sent to the Western Front, where he spent the rest of the war. He was not alone in his readiness to volunteer: a cutting from a local newspaper, preserved by his son, mentions that *several members of the rev. gentleman's church have joined Kitchener's Army*. Especially at the beginning, when it was widely thought that the war would be over in a few months, there was much popular enthusiasm for joining up among Nonconformist congregations in Wales, and even from the pulpit. A pacifist counter-argument was also preached, but it was the view of a small minority. Many more ministers of religion, though formally anti-war, felt called to extend their pastoral concern to the men who were fighting. Whatever the spirit that prompted them, once embroiled, army chaplains could not easily escape witnessing the dreadful consequences of trench warfare, even if they were not all like *old Evans the padre* in Wyn Griffith's UP TO MAMETZ, who, in the thick of the fighting, went *to bury other people's boys . . . since he couldn't find his own boy's grave to pray over*. Chaplains organized Sunday services in the lines, held communion on the field before battle, helped as best they could the wounded and dying, consoled the shell-shocked and bereaved, bowed their heads over the mass graves. Some or all of this, perhaps more, was Evan Mathias's experience; yet, when the war ended, he did not return to Pontypool Road Congregational Church but stayed with the army.

Early in 1920, his wife and two children joined him in Cologne, where he was stationed in the Chaplain General's office. He had a busy life and, while not one for the officers' mess, he participated in the army's social and leisure pursuits: a fine rugby-player, he captained the British Army of the Rhine Select XV. For his wife, travelling to Germany with two young children had been traumatic and, though comfortably enough housed, she was incapable of adjusting to the norms of existence for the wives of officers and ill-at-ease among the impoverished and resentful Germans. Holidays, which involved more travel, brought anxiety rather than relief.

In Cologne, their first home was the top floor of an elegant mansion in the suburb of Riehl. It overlooked the Rhine, and from the high window the young Roland Mathias watched for hours the passage of shipping. Much later this absorbing interest became the source of his short story 'The Rhine Tugs'. A year or so later they moved to well-appointed officers' quarters in Marienburg, another Cologne suburb. In both places, local girls were employed as servants and, through daily contact with them, the boy soon acquired a fair measure of proficiency in German. By his own account, at eight years of age he *spoke German fluently and knew far more of Hatto's Tower, of Charlemagne, of Eginhard and Emma* than he did of Wales. No Welsh was spoken in the home and his father's attempts to teach him Welsh were *desultory and short-lived*.

In 1923, the family returned to Britain, first to Southsea, where in October a daughter, Dilys, was born. With the death of Rachel Morgan in May 1920, a vital link with the Talybont area had been broken, so it was in the home of Mamgu, Evan Mathias's mother, in Llanelli, that they spent several weeks in the autumn of that year. Shortly before Christmas, a fresh posting, to Bulford Camp on Salisbury Plain, saw them settled in officers' quarters in the village, though some time later they moved to a hut on the perimeter of the camp. They were to stay in Bulford for some three and a half years, until the summer of 1926.

Muriel was no more reconciled to army life in England than she had been in Germany. She shunned the social round of officers' families and kept to her home where she was to her children the ever-present source of care and love. Their father was, by contrast, a distant, authoritarian figure, keen to encourage their best efforts in school, but inclined to impatience. In his ARTISTS IN WALES essay, Roland Mathias writes of *the exigencies of the wandering life we led from 1920 onwards.* It says much for the stability of the home that he coped with change and the timidity with which he claims he was afflicted as a child. He was a pupil first at the Black Watch (an army school) in Cologne, went to school in Llanelli for the six weeks or so the family spent there, and while in Bulford attended a private school in Amesbury which catered mostly for the children of officers, where the German so effortlessly acquired began to slip as easily away. *I learned to fear and dislike the two yardsticks by which the children of officers were measured, stature and social ease: by both, stuttering, undersized child that I was, I knew that I failed miserably,* he says of his school experience up to the age of eleven. But he was an avid reader and, whatever disadvantages he felt himself to have, he was clearly superior intellectually. When he was nine, his father gave him a second-hand copy of LONE TREE LODE by

Captain Owen Vaughan (Owen Rhoscomyl), a rousing western yarn first published in 1913, that he had inscribed: *To Roland . . . as a mark of appreciation of his first year's work at school. July 30th 1924.* This rare gift, the writer says, made him conscious that he was doing well at school and, more remarkably, that he had the distinction of being Welsh. The brief introduction to the book explains that it is a translation of letters written by one Dai Jeffreys to his mother in her farmhouse home *under the shoulder of the vast Pumluman mountain.* It has some curious references for a western, to the odes of Horace, Lyly's EUPHUES and More's UTOPIA, the last being of some significance in the narrative. Apart from the introduction, it says very little about Wales. Deep in the story (p.165), are the words *Me being Welsh,* which are the narrator's explanation of his sudden furious attack on *a great loose-jointed galoot* who sneered at his youth. It is not in the context of the book an unnecessary declaration, as Roland puts it in the ARTISTS IN WALES essay, but given the circumstances and the pride with which it is uttered, it is an assertion that might indeed stick in the mind of a small and studious boy. Be that as it may, the writer says these words evoked in him *a flutter of response. I had had my first introduction to Anglo-Welsh writing.*

In September 1925, Roland began his career as a boarder at Caterham School in Surrey. His initial contact with the school had been inauspicious: interviewed by the headmaster at the National Liberal Club in London, he was considered *not very bright.* He found at the school many other boys who, like him, were the sons of Welsh ministers. In his first year he was horribly afflicted with homesickness, but he survived and gradually settled.

From his time at Caterham, Roland Mathias has been a hoarder of magazines and papers of all kinds and an inveterate maker of scrap-books. Padded like cushions with their multitudinous contents, the old exercise books and ledgers that have been pressed to this service are piled high in his study. They testify to his curiosity about the natural world, humanity, religion and culture, and say a great deal about his personal story. It is perhaps the historian's method, the creation of an archive, though to the reader of them the image of geological strata may seem more appropriate as he descends through the layers of information.

Many of the details of the writer's life included in this essay are drawn from the scrap-books. One such is dedicated to extracts from the Caterham School magazine. It shows that he made rapid progress in his studies and was accelerated through several forms, winning prizes on the way. By the start of his third year he was well-established and beginning to make his mark in other aspects of school life. In 1929, while still not fourteen, he gained the London Matriculation, and in September of the same year he entered the sixth form. Here, as so often happens, his school career burgeoned. He had already con-tributed to the school magazine, now he wrote more frequently; he took part in debates, won a photo-graphic society prize and an honourable mention in a verse competition.

He continued top of his form but was prevented by the head from sitting the Higher School and Inter-mediate Arts examination in the summer of 1931 because he was considered too young. When in 1932 he sat the examination in history and French, he gained distinctions in both. Meanwhile he became a prefect (in due course senior prefect) and joint editor of the school magazine, gave papers to the Literary and Dramatic Society and made a considerable impact as an actor, playing both male and female parts. Familiar features of his later life were already emerging, along with the capacity to sustain and develop together a multiplicity of cultural interests with an abundance of energy and skill. Other traits less familiar to readers of the poetry and prose of Roland Mathias also emerged. As a sixth-former, although no longer the socially ill-at-ease stutterer of his early school-days, he was still undersized for his age. He nevertheless gave to rugby and hockey the same enthusiastic commitment he put into artistic pursuits, and won house colours in both. As a sportsman he was eclipsed by his brother Alun, who had followed him to Caterham in 1929 and was an outstanding performer in rugby, hockey and athletics. Roland, however, persisted with games, and the fearlessness the school magazine remarked in his falling on the ball at the feet of the opposing forwards has been manifest through his life in the way that he has faced challenges and stood his ground whenever moral and intellectual issues were at stake.

In his ARTISTS IN WALES essay Roland casts a disparaging glance back at his progress as a writer at Caterham: *In my Sixth Form days . . . I began to write with fluency in a highly-coloured romantic style . . . (that) came straight out of Tennyson and Arnold, with an argumentative muscle or two from Browning.* His English master commended its competence but did not like it. In his final term, however, the magazine reports that he won the Verse Prize *for a group of graceful lyrics.* At this stage, his writing is indeed as he and his English master assess it, but that is not surprising, nor were the models he chose inimical to the development of a poetic sensibility and, perhaps more important, the craft of poetry.

In his penultimate year at Caterham, a Christian journal, THE SUNDAY AT HOME, published an essay by Ronald (*sic*) G. Mathias (aged 17) in which he wrote, *For myself, I shall always ask for the same security in which I have been brought up – that peace and quiet which my home has always provided for me. This domestic security, which shows itself more on Sunday than on any other day of the week, is something of which I have always been certain.* In his unpublished memorial to his mother he says that even in his Oxford days, during vacations he did not go out in the evenings, unless it was very occasionally with the family. In this he resembled his mother, and the domestic security he referred to in his essay describes her love for her children and his relationship with her. The tensions between his mother and his father, however, persisted and worsened as her antipathy to the army deepened.

From 1926, home had been Aldershot where Evan Mathias, perhaps hoping for a more settled existence, bought a house. His wife occasionally served behind the counter of an army canteen but remained remote from its social life. In 1927, he spent the year in a tour of duty with the British Expeditionary Force to China, leaving behind a *perfectly self-sufficient family* and one son at least who, when he was at home, wanted nothing more than to stay there. By the time Roland was in his first year at Oxford, his father had been posted to Catterick and had rented a house in Richmond, on the edge of the Yorkshire moors. There the writer's mother was friendly with village neighbours, infinitely sympathetic and generous to those in need, but inflexible and ultimately unforgiving in her attitude to soldiering: her simple belief could not allow that patriotism bestowed the right to kill a fellow human. Any church that sanctioned an alternative view was unrighteous. Beyond that, her complete acceptance of God's will bordered on a fatalism that embraced herself and those she loved. Given the closeness of mother and son, it is inconceivable that he could remain unaffected by the strength of her beliefs.

Throughout this period, events in Europe gave alternately hope and presages of fresh horror, especially to those who had known the First World War and seen its aftermath. When in 1920 Muriel Mathias and her two young sons were travelling to Germany, the League of Nations was about to meet for the first time in Paris, though without many of the key players it needed to be a force for world peace. Shortly before the Mathias family returned from Germany in 1923, French and Belgian troops had occupied the Ruhr in an abortive effort to gain reparations from Germany and weaken her military strength for good, and in November of that year Hitler made a first attempt, also abortive, to wrest power from the elected government. At the height of the League of Nations' influence, in 1931, the NEWS CHRONICLE reported that fifteen prefects of Caterham School had signed the Peace Petition. By 1933, when Roland Mathias entered Jesus College, Oxford, Germany and Japan had withdrawn from the League and Hitler was chancellor of Germany.

At Oxford he read history and took his full share of the extra-curricular offerings of Jesus College. His college magazine scrap-book contains notes of the Sankey (debating) Society, the Meyricke (literary) Society, the Dramatic Society, the Rugby and Hockey Clubs, the Music Society, the Historical Society and the Henry Vaughan Society. One of the earliest collections of cuttings in a battered red exercise book (another of those with 'Danger Don'ts' on the back) includes a programme of the Dramatic Society's production of Aristophanes' THE BIRDS in which, prophetically, the part of A Poet is played by Roland Mathias – very well according to a review in THE OXFORD MAGAZINE. Other programmes show that he was president of the Dale Society (a Congregationalist fellowship) in 1935–6, and of the Historical Society in 1936–7. He won college colours in hockey and continued to play rugby, taking over as scrum-half in the college team early in the 1936–7 season. He became Jesus College correspondent to THE OXFORD MAGAZINE; to the Meyricke Society he gave a paper entitled 'Inspiration' on the nature and concept of poetry and, against his better judgement, was persuaded to submit, pseudonymously, to the college magazine poems that, like his school poems, have a Georgian or earlier ring and that he knew were *old hat*.

Academically he made rapid progress. He was awarded a Meyricke Exhibition in 1934 and a first-class Honours degree in history in 1936. With the degree result he won a college prize and among the books he bought with the prize money was Edith Sitwell's ASPECTS OF MODERN POETRY. This seems to have been a significant turning-point for him as a writer: it made him aware of *the concept of 'texture' in poetry and the conflict of ideas and attitudes in contemporary writing* and probably introduced him to the thinking of F. R. Leavis. His 'First' also brought election as an honorary scholar of the college and a £60 grant to undertake research. His thesis on 'The economic policy of the Board of Trade 1696–1714' (which he was later to present mockingly in the c.v. he supplied to the magazines of schools where he had been appointed headmaster as *still available, in typescript, for detention reading*) earned him the degree of Bachelor of Letters.

Jesus College in his day, Roland Mathias has said, was not as Welsh as it is now, nor was he *Welsh enough* to satisfy his tutor, Goronwy Edwards, but he spent his summers in Wales and was warmly welcomed by relatives from Llanelli in the west to the Rhondda and Sennybridge in the east. He discovered on these visits communities that, however deprived, were still close-knit, whole and wholesome. Responding to them, he began in these vacations an apprenticeship in writing that took as its starting-points landscape and history.

On a family holiday in Saundersfoot in the summer of 1938 he had other pressing concerns – the need to find a job, and worry about the increasing tension in Europe. Germany had for some time been rearming, had introduced conscription in 1935 and had occupied the Rhineland in 1936. In March 1938, Hitler seized Austria. In September 1938, Chamberlain met Hitler in Munich, returned bringing *peace with honour* and immediately launched a rearmament campaign. In the same month Roland Mathias was settling into his first teaching post, at Cowley School, St Helens, but he knew that, sooner now rather than later, he would face a religious and moral challenge the outcome of which would have profound repercussions for himself and his family, particularly his father.

At Cowley, a boys' grammar school, he was engaged on a temporary basis as acting senior history master and given a heavy teaching load. The scrap-book of the school's magazine, THE COWLEIAN, reveals the wide range of extra-curricular activities available to pupils and an emphasis on sport. With characteristic energy and enthusiasm, Roland gave much more to the school than his ability as a historian. In particular, he coached and played rugby, with considerable success. The St Helens rugby union club had begun as Old Cowleians (and for a time during the war reverted to that name and the school ground). Cuttings in the red exercise book follow the writer's progress from St Helens second XV to the first XV in January 1939. He played wing-forward and is frequently singled out in newspaper reports for his skill and tenacity. The next season had barely started when war was declared. Rugby cuttings are juxtaposed with war stories; the crisis he had long anticipated was imminent.

In June 1940 he appeared before the Lancashire and Cheshire Tribunal for Conscientious Objectors at St George's Hall, Liverpool, having applied for registration on religious grounds. A local newspaper reported that he told the tribunal: *The war is indefensible. He did not carry a gas mask. He would not take cover if a bomb fell (nor did he), because by so doing 'he would be taking part in the war effort'. It hurt his conscience to train children to go into air-raid shelters*. The last assertion, which was seized upon by columnists and correspondents to the newspaper, was to haunt him for a while. His statement to the tribunal, much of which the newspaper quotes verbatim, is logical (given his religious conviction), consistent and stubborn. The tribunal found against him and he was registered for *non-combatant duties*, that is, for duties in support of the war effort, albeit in a non-combatant role.

It became a *cause célèbre* in St Helens: the ratepayers were urged to demand that the Corporation sack him and all other conscientious objectors on its books. But he carried on teaching and his appointment was confirmed, by the chairman's casting vote, at a meeting of the Education Committee in March 1941. In the course of the meeting it transpired that, at his own suggestion, he had worked without pay since the previous September, following his unsuccessful appeal against registration for non-combatant duties.

Apart from being unpaid, his situation at the school remained much as before the tribunal. He was strongly supported by the headmaster, who was not himself a pacifist. Friendships in and out of school stood the test: in May 1941 he was best man at the wedding of a former teaching colleague and fellow member of the St Helens XV, who was by that time in the army. When the new season began in September 1941, he was still playing rugby, but in the same month he came to trial for refusing to attend a medical examination under the Armed Forces Act. The prosecutor asked for exemplary punishment. The Deputy Stipendiary Magistrate, however, decided against the full twelve-month penalty, imposing instead three months' imprisonment with hard labour. He served his sentence partly in Walton and partly in Stafford Gaol.

On receiving the summons to attend court, Roland Mathias had resigned his post at Cowley School.

When he left Stafford in November his position was the same as that before he went into prison: he had been registered for non-combatant duties and was directed to civil work. Instead, he applied for teaching posts and carried on playing rugby, with considerable success. A match report gave him a review that would bear comparison with any of his later literary successes:

Outstanding in the Cowleians set [of forwards] was Mathias. Even in this topsy-turvy world, one scarcely expects to find a pacifist in a rugby pack.

All who knew him respected his pacifism and supported him in his stand. Much good had come from the St Helens experience and he emerged from it, if not entirely unscathed, his own man, confirmed in his convictions and sure of himself.

In January 1942 he began teaching at the Blue Coat School in Reading, a boys' grammar of ancient foundation. That was not the end of the story as far as the authorities were concerned. In October of that year and again in November he was instructed to proceed to work at the Great Western Railway in Didcot. He refused, because his conscience would not permit him to take employment that would release another man to join the war effort, and he was summonsed to appear before the Reading Borough Police Court early in December. Ordered to pay a £20 fine or go to prison for three months, he chose prison. On this occasion his incarceration was brief; on 20 December he was released from HM Prison, Oxford, on payment of the balance of the fine by the boys and staff of the Blue Coat School. He had made many friends in his short time at the school.

He was not alone in the strength of his Christian belief and certainty that adherence to that belief was incompatible with any form of participation in the war effort. He was not the only pacifist among Welsh writers. He was probably unique, however, in having a father who had dedicated much of his life to the army. When Evan Mathias had retired in 1940, it was as colonel and the longest-serving chaplain of the 'United Board' (the combined Free Churches). He and his wife had returned from Catterick to Aldershot in 1934. Now the house in Aldershot was sold and a new home bought in a familiar place – Brecon. This renewal of old ties brought no balm. The writer's mother was as adamant in her beliefs as ever. Trust in God alone was needed: the churches that condoned war, and even the evacuation of children, were unchristian. Unlike their neighbours in England, the people of Brecon took an interest in her unusual views and did not approve of them, but her puritanism was not susceptible to persuasion, nor to argument nor to brow-beating (and in this her son resembled her). While she stayed indoors, however, Evan Mathias endured the disapprobation of chapel-goers and townspeople. Although his army days were over, there could be no peace between them while the war lasted. It must have seemed to him also that his son's hopeful career in education was irreparably damaged, but that was not so.

In addition to Roland's firm hold on principle, his determination to teach, his continuing to play rugby, there was in 1942 a further demonstration that he had come through the experience of tribunals, courts and imprisonment: he published his first book of poems. Although in format it appears so, DAYS ENDURING is not a slim volume. It contains sixty-one poems, a few from his time at Caterham, but most from the period 1935 to 1942. The poems appear to be printed in the order in which they were written, but the chronological arrangement is inexact. No other mode of organization is obvious. The great majority rhyme and many are in regular, often complex, though not traditional, stanza forms. They are the work of a writer who delights in the craft of poetry. All are highly wrought and there are very few that do not have a strikingly felicitous image or turn of phrase to delight the mind and ear.

His models are the Romantic and Victorian poets (Keats and Tennyson come readily to mind) but also, possibly, contemporaries like de la Mare and Masefield. The diction is nineteenth-century poetic: tears are *jewelled*; the sun is *o'erlain with clouds*; a place can be *A paradise enow . . . embalmed new from Lethe's pool*; *unnoticed* rhymes with *dead*. There are clichés and archaisms enough to prompt the thought of parody, but the imitation flatters without irony. These are the poems of a young man trying his strength as a writer, full to the brim with words, as one would expect of an avid reader with a tenacious memory and no small gift for self-dramatization. His imagery is influenced far less by observation than by reading. Landscape and location are expressed by generalities; personification and pathetic fallacy are common features. His eye is frequently cast up to observe the sun, the clouds and stars; he is a poet of weathers, especially the turbulent sort. Religious themes and images are rare. Perhaps, like Ruskin, he believed that, because God created the natural world, to depict nature was to praise God; no more overt reference was needed.

Frequently, his inspiration is in contrasts – of town

and country, calm and storm, past and present. Time is a common theme, most obviously in poems that mark the New Year, in 1935, 1936 and 1939, but curiously detached from world events. The depression, the rise of fascism and of communism, the Spanish Civil War leave no mark on his poetry. 'Rissersee' and 'Knapweed', written after a visit to Bavaria with an Oxford friend in the summer of 1935, are about landscape and recollection of time past, his childhood in Germany. For much of the book the historian and the pacifist are dissociated from the poet, but as the catastrophe in Europe and his personal crisis approach, they come together into focus. At the same time, it seems, the influence of Edith Sitwell's analysis of modern poetry emerges in poetic forms that are more flexible, and in utterance more 'textured' and more concentrated. Above all, his poetry becomes more direct in its observation of life. As with other writers of the period, combatant or not, the war developed sinew in the poetry of Roland Mathias.

The change occurs abruptly. 'New Year 1939' is full of vague foreboding; in 'Lines Written on Hearing of the Invasion of Poland (September 1st, 1939)', in a style that differs little from his earlier writing, he faces the prospect of the extinction of all his plans, but with 'Declaration of War (September 3rd, 1939)' a new bitterness accompanies description of the first moments of war, as he observed them, ironically it must have seemed for one who was a pacifist, in Aldershot.

> The man next door
> Lay last night through in Oudenarde,
> The barracks over hill, and phoned his wife

> *That it was quite a lark, a change*
> *From civil crawlings to and fro . . . A change?*
> *Why not? . . . He has no option now*
> *On English earth, no hour to choose*
> *His seven feet for air and light and view*
> *Towards the park. He'll find he has*
> *No rights at all against the massing worms*
> *That violate his frontier.*

A group of six poems conveys the experience of prison. The first, in the order that they appear in the book, 'Inter Tenebros (Even Here)', is an affirmation of faith:

> *Here in the pit, the nether lines*
> *I feel Thy penetration,*
> *Lord.*

Like 'Vista' and 'Bars', the two that follow, it displays technical virtuosity in its structure and use of rhyme. But all three poems are different in character from the polished verses that fill most of the book. This is not a product of subject matter alone, but of the controlled feeling that pervades them. Compared with these, the earlier poems are exercises, often highly skilled, but empty of emotion. The prison images, too, strike hard, whether simple (*night is a ten-paned vault of black*) or complex with metaphysical wit, like the *seven-squared days that bleach and crack / Between the walls and balconies* in the two highly wrought stanzas of 'Bars'.

References to Wales come frequently enough in DAYS ENDURING. They occur among the earlier poems, occasionally unattributed (some unspecified rural settings are clearly Welsh), but more often place-names are used to conjure up nostalgia or point a

21

contrast with England: Sir Benfro, Teifi, the Beacons in 'Hiraeth', for example. In 'Evening in Saundersfoot', which has a complex rhyming stanza form reminiscent of early narrative verse by Auden (and deserves to be as frequently anthologized), he describes a strange encounter, perhaps with smugglers, on the darkening sands. 'On Newport Reservoir', however, foreshadows the mature writing of Roland Mathias. Its theme, the drowning of the valley where his grandparents farmed, was one to which he would return.

In three poems towards the end of the book, he draws spiritually closer to Wales. It is no longer just a place of relatives and holidays, but resonates with his own beliefs and his sense of history. It has a social order to which he responds and people with whom he feels at home. 'Maesyronnen' re-creates within the 300-year-old dilapidated chapel the congregations and stern Nonconformity of earlier times. 'Pastorale' describes a bus journey from Merthyr by the Cefn road to Brecon and the people who shared it, and 'Balloon over the Rhondda' the destruction of a fly-away barrage balloon by fighter aircraft as chapel-goers make their way to Tabor. The latter ends with the unselfconscious benediction of an aged deacon:

> *he said*
> *'I hope you'll set the world to rights, my son'*
> *And plodded on.*
> *Under the sky they were the dumb who nodded.*

A year or so later, Keidrych Rhys selected 'Balloon over the Rhondda' for his anthology MODERN WELSH POETRY (1944). Here Roland Mathias found himself for the first time in the company of Idris Davies, Alun Lewis, David Jones, Emyr Humphreys, Vernon Watkins, Ormond Thomas (John Ormond), R. S. Thomas and Dylan Thomas, whose work would become his study, and with some of whom he was to share in the upsurge of Anglo-Welsh writing in the 1960s.

Roland's long and painstaking service as an editor began in Reading towards the end of the war. He was by this time married to Mary Annie (Molly) Hawes, daughter of an Oxfordshire farming family. The wedding, in April 1944, followed less than a year after that of Alun Mathias to Molly's first cousin Dorothy, also of farming stock. The brothers were best man at each other's weddings and their father officiated with the local pastor at the ceremonies. Roland and Molly Mathias settled in Reading, where both were teaching. They were active in the Congregational church and in clubs and societies. Reading, even in the war years, had a diverse and rather rich cultural life of its own. With a friend, Pierre Edmunds, Roland started a magazine called HERE TODAY that was intended to contribute directly to that life.

While it cast its critical net widely and looked far afield for creative writing, the magazine's stated aim was to publish local writers and review events in the region. Three numbers appeared under the joint editorship, the first and second in June and October 1944, the third in March 1945. They all differ slightly in format and appearance; none is dated. Editorial comment inevitably focused on the war, but also on the prospect for social improvement when it was over. Notes on the theatre point to Roland's interest in acting. He and the novelist Elizabeth Taylor, who was just beginning to be recognized, were the most notable contributors. In addition to articles on local events like 'promenade concerts', there were poems, short stories and reviews. It was a small venture, but modestly successful, a model worth replicating.

Roland Mathias's contributions to HERE TODAY are varied and substantial. They include three poems, all in the first number. Among them, 'Kidmore End', with its echoes of Edward Thomas and of the conversational tone of Robert Frost, shows what he had learned from ASPECTS OF MODERN POETRY about texture.

> *I remember agrimony. And the tall*
> *Woolly yellow plant you said you thought*
> *Was mullein, shouldering*
> *The small brushed space behind*
> *The cornfield, and the slope,*
> *The sudden slanting of the perilous ears*
> *Crowding the slattern fence*
> *We climbed to reach the copse . . .*

Contemporary readers might think Edith Sitwell's ear too sensitive to vowels and to consonants, or that she does not persuade them of the effect they had on her, when she writes (apropos W. H. Davies) of a *long, dewy 'qu' . . . the deeper, dipping sound of 'water' . . . the shining sound of 'skates'*. None the less, she demonstrates texture in terms that are familiar, as those sound effects, especially alliteration, assonance and internal rhyme, allied to variations in the pattern of stresses and the placement of the caesura, that have been taken to characterize Welsh writing in English. The proliferation of 'l' and 's' sounds in the lines above from 'Kidmore End' is obvious enough, but there is subtlety, too, in the patterning of vowel sounds and the peculiarly apt and punning choice of 'slattern' to describe the fence.

The second number of HERE TODAY included the short story 'Block-System', collected later in THE ELEVEN MEN OF EPPYNT, and the third an impressive article entitled 'The Mental Invalid and the Modern Novel', in which Roland set out an approach to criticism consistent with his Christian belief and morality that has not changed. He quotes with approval V. S. Pritchett on George Eliot, *orderly in her ethics . . . orderly in her social observation . . . showing how the minds of characters must be placed among other minds.* In words that presage the pronouncements of a more renowned critic he observes: *Perhaps we should relish the achievement of the classical realists over and over again in the fear that a great tradition has really ended.*

In February 1945, Molly Mathias gave birth to twins. His responsibilities thus enlarged, Roland applied himself to the task of furthering his career in teaching. In this too he was characteristically energetic. In July 1945, he left the Blue Coat School and took his family north to Carlisle. His post as senior history master at Carlisle Grammar School for Boys was temporary, pending the return of staff from war service, but he quickly established himself as a teacher of distinction and a ready contributor to extra-curricular activities. He supported the Debating Society, coached rugby football and joined enthusiastically in the tradition of staff participation in Dramatic Society productions.

In September 1946, he took up a new appointment on the permanent staff of another boys' grammar school, St Clement Dane's Holborn Estate, which was actually located near Wormwood Scrubs in London. Here too, he found an acting tradition and performed in school and staff productions. In his second year at the school he joined the group of staff that accompanied boys on an annual 'harvest camp' at Standlake, a few miles west of Oxford, and brought to this experience the same high spirits he had shown at similar camps for the boys of Cowley School. Subsequently, he contributed an introductory prose piece to the camp souvenir magazine, and a poem, 'Camp by the Windrush', that also appeared in THE LISTENER.

The professional demands of school and those, largely self-imposed, of rugby coaching, amateur dramatics and the like, were not allowed to stand in the way of his writing. Having begun to find his voice as a poet, he wrote constantly and was frequently published, in England (Tambimuttu's POETRY LONDON and OUTPOSTS), and in Wales (THE WELSH REVIEW and Keidrych Rhys's WALES).

His return to the south of England had coincided with the publication in 1946 of his second volume of poetry, BREAK IN HARVEST. The poems in this book are closely linked in time and place. The great majority were written between 1943 and 1945; the last, 'Going', a graphic account of moving house and the memories of childhood it evokes, marks the family's transfer north to Carlisle in the summer of 1945.

'Balloon over the Rhondda' (which like 'Pastorale' was also included in DAYS ENDURING) and 'The Cauldron of Diwrnach Wyddel' are in their different ways poems of the war. The latter uses the story from THE MABINOGION and reference to recent and historical events to raise the issue of cowardice and moral courage that, as the campaigns in Europe were drawing to a close, had for the moment a fresh significance. 'In This Cold Room', 'Requiescat' and the title poem contain passing or indirect allusions to the war; in 'Lowbury Hill', though there are *tank tracks* on the landscape, it is stirringly alive with Arthurian battles. The poet-historian had put aside contemporary conflict.

The major themes of the book are love, family and Wales, especially Breconshire. The poems of love are also about places in the contrasting landscape of Oxfordshire, in and around Fulwell Farm, near Enstone, where his wife was brought up. The habit of history leads the poet to see everywhere features and figures of the past. In 'For M.A.H.' the lovers' Cotswold landscape has a fourth dimension:

> *Walls cannot hold the wind against me now:*
> *I am the one to walk the rows at Tew*
> *Believing jasmine breathes the shape of you*
> *And Lucius Cary makes you his first bow.*

> *I am with Hampden in his ragged charge*
> *Hoping for Chiselhampton held or down:*
> *I ride with Bushell into Oxford town*
> *To mint the college loyalty in large.*

It recalls metaphysical poetry and is indeed metaphysical, re-creating the seventeenth century in the present. Bushell appears again in the poem 'Enstone Rock' as the student and follower of Bacon and mining engineer, who earned from Charles I *the grant/Of mines in silver Wales* that are the subject of the later short story, 'Digression into Miracle'. For all the historical detail, characteristic muscular writing and the apostrophizing theatrical device, this too is a love poem celebrating in the present *you, your loveliness.*

'Fulwell' is a passionately extended image of a well that reflects the moon in its depths and waits for the drawer.

> *I move. I am still, rather.*
> *Only the moonlight heaved.*
> *The quiet is yours . . .*
>
> *Come, I am moveless.*
> *Come gather me, waiting*
> *The winter for drawing, the deep for taking*
> *The moon up in heartfuls . . .*

Through the elaborate conceits and private reference of 'Last Happiness' the lovers are glimpsed, hanging on, in the *whirring days*, finding momentary comfort together and parting again. The countryside west of Reading, the village of Sulham, not far from Pangbourne, is the setting of 'Crossing into Peace'. This latter poem is easier in mood and less complex in expression. The events of its summer day

> *were part*
> *Of memory. The high banks had been*
> *Years that had grown there on the heart*
> *And the Pang between.*

The simplicity of the four-line rhyming stanza, and of the pun in the last line, are in contrast to poems in which metrical invention is allied to complexity of thought and imagery. For 'Last Happiness' the poet creates a five-line stanza which has a regular pattern of end and internal rhymes:

> *In the wet pageantry tonight deploys*
> *For answer to my calling joys, I write*
> *A parting in the head of midnight's hair*
> *And picture it, there white*
> *And straight as daylight on the dress you wear.*

This development of texture is a major advance in BREAK IN HARVEST. It reaches its apotheosis with one of several poems of rural England, in the main Oxfordshire, which stand alongside the love poems. In 'Evening: Unloading Wheat', the two five-line stanzas have end rhymes, rhymes that link the first word of the first line with the last of the second, and the second syllable of the fourth line with the last of the fifth. The stanzas too are linked by rhymes at the end of the fourth line.

> *Sesame, word of logic, or wild guess*
> *Towards this mandate's golden-brown economy,*
> *Open my hand with magic, work no less*
> *Than Mars with this so-grainèd weapon*
> *To build unanswerable hours beyond the wars.*

The exigencies of this pattern make for obscurity in particulars, though the general meaning is clear. Early reviewers remarked the difficulty of the poetry without acknowledging its technical virtuosity; yet Roland is one of the most painstaking metrical craftsmen in contemporary literature.

'Grace Before Work' links the poems of rural England with another group about the countryside of

Wales and his father's family, whose roots lay in the more grudging soil of Carmarthenshire. The poem takes as its starting-point a reiteration of Forster's *Only connect* . . . but in a spirit of self-admonition:

> *Then in remembering I do not enough*
> *To integrate the present with the past.*

The poet is the undeserving beneficiary of the labour of the previous generations of *dark, long-headed men*. He must serve as remembrancer of their toil and their simple Christianity, so that they share in the richer present, or else *go home/No more*. Home in 'The Bearers' is Breconshire, in the shadow of the Beacons:

> *Yet I am home*
> *With handgrip, knowing*
> *Something there is that turns me to the hills . . .*

This love of place is hard, devoid of sentiment or prettiness. The red ploughed soil, wet or frosted, or (in 'Subite') the untrodden snow covering *the mort of leaves . . . reek/Of the unswept past* are the character-istically wintry images of Wales in this book.

BREAK IN HARVEST attracted little critical attention. It is a challenging book, and it deserves to be recog-nized as a bridge between Roland Mathias's earliest published poetry and his fully mature writing – which is foreshadowed in many individual poems. Here he is testing his technical virtuosity and estab-lishing themes and attitudes. What he described elsewhere as *a yearning affinity for Wales* is already an inspiration, and he is emerging as a remarkable interpreter of landscape, often seeing it layered with history. The concentration of love poems and the strong association with rural Oxfordshire would not be repeated. The final poem, 'Going', is full of the sense of closed chapters, boyhood, adolescence and young manhood concluded, and a new beginning beckoning. He sees himself and his family

> out on a tangent from the torn circle
> Of friends, projected towards infinity . . .

As in art, so it was in life.

II

In his second year at St Clement Dane's, Roland applied for the post of headteacher at Pembroke Dock Grammar School. He was approaching thirty-three and had been teaching for nine years or so at four different boys' grammar schools in England, to each of which he had given a great deal. Those short-listed with him were older and more experienced in the profession, but his academic qualifications and teaching credentials were outstanding. His father's fears that his gaol sentence as a conscientious objector would be held against him were not realized; when it came to being interviewed, he was, as the Revd L. Alun Page, then minister of the Congregational church in Pembroke Dock, wrote much later in TALIESIN, *y creadur o ddyn mwyaf 'articulate' a adnabum erioed* ('the most articulate man I ever knew'). He got the job.

When the Mathias family arrived in Pembroke Dock in the summer of 1948, they found a town that, although small and economically depressed, was culturally lively. Its chapels were well attended and had their own varied societies; it had an Arts Club and two amateur dramatic societies. In the hinterland there were regular eisteddfodau at which competition went on well into the night. In short, it offered Roland many opportunities to use his talents as an actor, speaker and writer. He took them all. His energy was prodigious and he set high standards, for himself and others. The first change of policy at the school to attract the attention of the local press was his resolution, soon after his arrival, to change the major winter game from soccer to rugby football. When a reporter called to ask why, he found the headmaster coaching boys on the newly designated rugby pitch.

In the spring of 1949, a little later in that first year at Pembroke Dock, he came to a decision that was to have a far-reaching influence on Welsh writing in English. As his first staff appointment, he made the recently graduated Raymond Garlick assistant English master. Looking back on this event in an article in PLANET (number 9), Raymond Garlick writes of Roland Mathias as *one of the youngest and most brilliant headmasters in Wales at that time*. Of the origins of DOCK LEAVES he says: *The magazine was founded out of a group of people who met regularly to discuss literature, but the impetus that transformed it from a project to a reality was supplied by Roland Mathias . . . (The punning name 'Dock Leaves' was his suggestion . . .).*

The first number appeared under Raymond Garlick's editorship in the autumn of 1949. Both he and Roland have at various times emphasized that the continuation of the magazine required the dedication of a small team of supporters, especially as it survived without subsidy from the Arts Council until number 31 (by which time it had been renamed THE ANGLO-WELSH REVIEW). The name of Morwyth Rees, treasurer of the magazine for many years, stands high with both, but there were several others, most having a connection with the school. Olwen Rees was wife of the history master, Nora Davies a school governor and Anne Lewis Davies senior mistress of the school; William Smith, who later became circulation manager, was an old boy. There were also the Revd Alun Page and Henry Birkhead, *a retired Foreign Office classicist* – and Glyn Walters of H. G. Walters & Co., the magazine's printers from number 3 in 1950 to its demise with number 88 in 1988.

Pembroke Dock Grammar School was the focus of both the literary interest and the fund-raising activities that sustained the magazine. Gifts were received from several local sources, such as the Pembroke Dock Dramatic Society, and a sixth-form carol-singing party, all acknowledged with much gratitude in various numbers, but it came to rely on the proceeds of an annual autumn sale of work, usually held in the school hall, the first of which took place in 1953.

The history of DOCK LEAVES–ANGLO-WELSH REVIEW deserves a monograph of its own, and must be a constant theme in this essay because it is so closely bound up with Roland Mathias's own story. He was not only the prime mover of DOCK LEAVES, but its constant inspiration – and more than that, by far the largest and most consistent contributor. His work is to be found in all but two of the twenty-two numbers. Frequently he is represented by several pieces, poetry and prose, in a single issue.

Roland Mathias's third book, THE ROSES OF TRETOWER, published in 1952, is almost entirely the product of the years 1946 to 1951. It includes a group of poems from his brief sojourn in Carlisle, recognizable by their settings of sea and mountain and by the gazetteer of their titles. In the same way, a few are identifiably Oxfordshire poems, but the great majority have their genesis in Wales, Breconshire and Pembrokeshire, including six that were published in the first three numbers of DOCK LEAVES.

The mature style that had begun to emerge with the prison poems and developed in BREAK IN HARVEST was by 1949 well-established, as was the poet's voice – cultured, a little pedantic, authoritative, predisposed to melancholy, but witty. The poet's voice and the voices of other men, from other times and places, speaking through him, sometimes merge, as in 'A Letter'. There is no preamble to these poems, the speaker (or writer) is not introduced and the reader is drawn into the drama as silent interlocutor. Here the tone is brusque:

> *Eight years ago come Tuesday now I walked*
> *Big as a brown wind angry from your door.*
> *Mad you had made me, Ellen Skone, talked*
> *My tongue out of duty, crossed me more*
> *That day than I remember. And the sun came down*
> *Like a bakestone. Well, that was it!*

It is a manner typical of a lover of the theatre and acting, and evocative of the metaphysical poets of the seventeenth century, especially Donne, but also Henry Vaughan who was to become one of several continuing quests in the writer's life. In 'A Letter', and in later similar poems, the voice has a note of irritability that is distinctive, as this poetic mode distinguishes Roland Mathias among contemporary poets.

'Remember Charlie Stones, Carpenter' has a permanent place in Anglo-Welsh writing. A contemplation on life and dissolution before a commemorative tablet, elegantly lettered by Eric Gill, at Capel-y-ffin, it is a curiously hesitant personal manifesto for a staunchly Christian poet.

The stream is sultry and a short haze mulls it,
I in the hooved earth merry as a stick
Half-peeled and giving the horse-turds ample berth.
Here, having eaten, what in hysteria can I do
But wait, as shell and paper wait, myself
The best time to be thrown away?

In the coining of images, in the diction with its occasional archaisms (*prating as ill as I*), and in the flexibility of its rhythm that imitates the natural stresses of conversational English, it is strongly representative of the writer's art. The ambivalence of the concluding lines is also characteristic:

Are you bound there, Charlie? By one or many?
Rattle the church-box louder and detect my penny.
I know too well to remember, Charlie Stones, carpenter.

Landscape, the seasons and the weather, especially the wind, were from the first prominent in Roland Mathias's poetry. 'O Tihuanaco' (which draws on Aztec mythology) begins *I have prayed askance in the slow cold air* and the god's answer is made manifest in a natural world that is benign or malignant. Weather informs the imagery of human emotions in 'A Letter' – *I walked/Big as a brown wind angry from your door*. The meditation on death in 'Remember Charlie Stones, Carpenter' is set in a recognizable Gwent landscape in August heat. In 'A Winter's Day', *A puff of smoke pulls the wind about*.

'Morning: New Jerusalem' is another study of mortality. It is not, like 'Charlie Stones', a personal poem, but an animadversion on gossips' morbid interest in the impending death of a neighbour. In it the poet employs his dramatic skills with satirical purpose, but at its heart is an authorial recognition that

> *Beyond the wall and the curtains meeting*
> *Against infinity there is no choice*

which has a hint of that doubt or dissatisfaction with
the human condition that the memorial tablet at
Capel-y-ffin inspired.

Many of the poems in THE ROSES OF TRETOWER are
recognizably the work of a deeply religious poet, but
one to whom faith does not come easily and pious-
ness not at all. There is much darkness and question-
ing in the book. 'The Mountain' (one of those from
Carlisle) sounds the keynote:

> *I have been here in the fields a year*
> *And never felt so far, desperately*
> *Far from the course of Christ*
> *And of His star.*

He is honest and hard in his analysis of personal fail-
ings. It is the daily round of getting and spending
that prevents the healing spring reaching the *arid
spirit's pride*. In thought and imagery which, in the
same setting, connect with those of Wordsworth and
Ruskin, he sees in the mountain rising over the flat
lands of the firth, a *still pointer from despond*, a guarantee of the Godhead and life everlasting. In a climax close-knit with that patterning of sounds that
had become his signature, the poet prays

> *O I am growing old and would have word*
> *Of more than gossamer and graves;*
> *Give me the punishment that saves,*
> *A mountain ministry, appraising Lord . . .*

Few of the landscapes in these poems offer solace in
themselves. They tend to be harsh and windswept,

autumnal or wintry; growth is never far from rot, nor life from death. Frost stiffens the red, churned soil, the petals of Easter flowers fall like blood, the feathers of a dead bird barely move in a thin stream, a hawk, *irate as a stone*, hovers above the hill, the lamb the children find is eyeless. For a Christian, seeing life plain demands unblinking recognition of mortality, service and a readiness to respond whenever called. In the darker poems these conditions chafe; even in the parable of the flowers 'In Offenham Church' there is a hint of less than perfect satisfaction:

> *For the proud generation taken in its bloom*
> *There is still no resurrection, only sudden*
> *Demand and service, the dropped heart on the floor.*

Prospects of consolation can be deceptive. 'Evening' begins serenely –

> *Cool is the plot of evening, consolation*
> *Is pressed out of the currant leaves*

– but the ambiguity of *plot* is confirmed in the final lines:

> *This is the part of evening, that the rotten*
> *Stales and refreshes not, feeding on no heart's blood.*

'Freshwater West' is another dark poem. Against the incessant beat of breaking waves, conveyed in the densely textured verse by rhythm, alliteration and onomatopoeia, the poet contemplates obliteration. Here he is not what he must have appeared to others, self-assured, successful, pushing ahead with energy and intellect, but prey to doubt and self-doubt. He wishes *Only for peace*, and the sea's answer is among the most nihilistic in Roland Mathias's writing:

> *Of your half wish there is nothing lost,*
> *Nothing of praise and success, over*
> *And over spoken, nothing but gland*
> *And flesh, a rushing atomiser*
> *Broken like sand from off the human coast.*

The drowned valley of Glyn Collwn is the subject of two elegiac poems, 'The Flooded Valley' and 'Returning'. A few details in the former, which appear also in the short story 'Ffynnon Fawr', are from his father's account of a visit to the ruins of the poet's birthplace, then at the water's edge, but it is essentially an impassioned complaint to the rivers that were once companionable, in the name of the families (his own forebears) that the reservoir has driven away.

'Returning' has far more circumstantial detail, because the observations it contains are those of the poet himself. Personal history evokes a perception of time as the focus of place pulls together present and past. Remembrance of childhood, always acute in Roland's writing, is lent particular poignancy by the presence of his own children who have accompanied him in his exploration. Unexpectedly, however, these are incidentals. The poem is about self-analysis, self-doubt, self-depreciation and, with the emergence of this theme, the character of the verse changes. The patterning of sound, though subtle, becomes dense and persistent to the final rhyming lines:

If the whole dusk of fears
And the missioner's box mounting the feathered lane with me
Slight and shrinking at bole or bush or the eared shadow of a
  fox
Slinking, survive in the vile push rotating
The seen half of my world, behind o
Beyond the last wile in the covert, the eyeless lamb
(Was it an eagle, was it, was it?), overt
In shoot and stem God's very hosts groan in mid-shock.
Blood out of them unreds the rock.

Images of vegetation as insidious and conspiratorial echo the narrative of the young woman who deceives her father to tryst with her lover in the title poem. The long line, commoner in this book than those that preceded it, colloquialisms, sardonic humour and irony, and the texturing of the rhyming stanzas make a simple rural love story as knotted and thorny as an untended rose bush.

At the heart of the book lies a group of poems, several of which explore the same themes, that find inspiration in Breconshire and the border. Perhaps the most important of these is 'Remember Charlie Stones, Carpenter', which has its shadows of ambiguity and doubt, but among them are three poems that are clear in their expression of Christian faith. 'Olchon' is a refutation of doubt, exalting instead *the child's/Wide trust* that picks the true path to Christ. In 'Drought', the river scene contains images of death – the still carcass in the stream, the dipper *like an undertaker* and the cloud of flies, but it is a picture of *the supreme/Insufficiency of death*. 'On the Grave of Henry Vaughan at Llansaintffraed' concludes with a paean of affirmation in which the poet's mound overlooks the promised land and is fitted for flight:

Man that is God and ghost, fuel and fire,
Factor and master, ephemeral, crossed
Peccator maximus *stirring to desire,*
Dust shall have shape and sing, in the sun faster –
This hump is Pisgah and each shoulder wing!

THE ROSES OF TRETOWER was little reviewed. Remarks about the obscurity of poems appeared in a few brief notices. In a local Pembrokeshire newspaper, Waldo Williams also noted occasional difficulties, but recognized in the book the work of a poet *with a brooding interest in the human predicament.* Disheartened by the more general apathy, Roland sought the advice of fellow writers, Gwyn Jones and Glyn Jones. They had none to offer: metropolitan reviewers wrote about their circle of acquaintance and Wales was off their map. Both, however, saw in this volume the work of a true poet with a distinctive voice. This brought some satisfaction, but the experience bred in him a chronic mistrust of the London-based literary press, and a determination to give Welsh writers the benefit of serious, critical consideration in a respected journal – a task he had already taken upon himself in reviewing for DOCK LEAVES.

Most writers have done their share of reviewing – some for the pittance it brought in, many more simply because an editor asked. A few have dedicated a good part of their lives to it, raised it to a form of art and made a significant contribution to literature in commenting on the new work of contemporaries, often because their response is revealingly personal. Roland Mathias is an assiduously expert reviewer who reveals in his reviews his Nonconformist Christian belief, a code that leads him to the conclusion that literature should implicitly convey clear moral standards.

The reviews do not mince words, but there is no smartness, no gratuitous scoring of points at the expense of the writer. Though often illuminated with imagery – some unexpectedly drawn from boxing, hunting and horse racing – the writing is mostly sober in tone, as befitted the majority of the books on which he turned his scholarly searchlight.

For one who was not, after all, a professional historian, he was in his reviews a remarkable contributor to studies in Welsh history. He gave time, care and space to his observations on books that normally attracted little attention or publicity, and he set high standards. He is sharp on shortcomings of any kind, from poor editing and the absence of maps to inaccuracies and omissions. His own wide reading and prodigious memory are frequently revealed as he takes authors to task. Professors of history are shown the cause of their error in confusing characters who bear the same name, criticized for not following a line of enquiry to a proper conclusion, or referred to sources that could have filled out their inadequate treatment of the Welsh contribution to the development of the United States, a subject he found fascinating. He takes issue with archaeologists for making authoritative statements about dates that he knows still to be in doubt, puts the hypothesis of one historian of the Celtic saints against another and draws his own conclusion, and dismisses as unworthy the selection of Robert Roberts ('Y Sgolor Mawr') as the subject of a book for children aged eleven to thirteen, because of his other reputation as a drinker.

Morality, fitness for purpose, essential goodness are central concerns adopted as part of his critical apparatus and applied consistently from the article on the modern novel in HERE TODAY and throughout his career as reviewer and critic. Henry Treece's early novels are criticized not only for distorting Welsh history and tradition, but also for their graphic depiction of brutality; Thom Gunn's poetry is admired for its technique but censured because it is uninvolved, depersonalized, deficient in feeling. The small band of writers that Roland Mathias regularly reviewed was already forming. Its members all have something to say about man in relation to God and nature and a strong sense of place. Although he thought them worthy of a wider readership than they enjoyed, this did not imply any diminution of his critical faculty when it came to reviewing them. Thus, while he states plainly that John Cowper Powys is a great writer, all four Powys novels reviewed in DOCK LEAVES are judged unsuccessful and disappointing. Vernon Watkins's THE DEATH BELL is *not . . . particularly interesting*, and of Emyr Humphreys's A MAN'S ESTATE he registers *disappointment . . . in terms of the author's purpose*, although the book is *a gripper*. His dissatisfaction with the latter arises from an earlier recognition that, like him, Humphreys has strong Nonconformist principles and seeks to express in his writing Christian morality. The outcome of the novel does not show, to the reviewer's satisfaction, the moral change at work.

John Cowper Powys and Vernon Watkins are also the subjects of articles Roland Mathias wrote for DOCK LEAVES. That on Watkins (number 3, 1950) pays generous tribute to him as a master of poetic form second only to Eliot among contemporaries, but sees his conception of art as detached from the experience of life and peculiarly sterile – *I feel . . . that Watkins has succeeded in doing what I thought could never be done: he has depersonalised Wales.* In Dylan Thomas's poems in THE MAP OF LOVE, he saw not Wales but the deleterious influences of London and lionization. This view appears in the article he wrote for the special issue of DOCK LEAVES to mark Thomas's death (number 13, 1954) that balances Thomas's impressive achievement against the failures of spiritual development and poetic intention in the downright bad poems in the middle section of the COLLECTED POEMS. His analysis also shows what few, if any, critics had previously recognized: Thomas's deep knowledge of English literature and the extent to which many of the poems are constructed by word association and *dictionary hunting.*

For the John Cowper Powys special (number 19, 1956) he provides a bold, rhetorical article critical of the novelist's ability to develop character, write convincing dialogue, describe a recognizable human society, while still acknowledging his unique strength in conveying the spirit of vegetation and a sense of history and place. These qualities explain Roland's continuing interest in Powys, despite the declining powers he had remarked in his critical reviews of the later books. He looked for a similar sense of place in Henry Vaughan's writing and did not find it. Vaughan is another member of the critic's personal pantheon. The attraction in this case came of connections they shared – Jesus College (where he attended meetings of the Henry Vaughan Society) and Breconshire where he was born and had family roots. In giving readers 'A glimpse of Henry Vaughan's Breconshire' (number 7, 1952), he remarked the apparent paradox that, although Vaughan proclaimed himself a Welshman and clearly knew the landscape well, his descriptions of it are few and vaguely generalized. The reasons lie, fairly obviously, in his time, his classical education, metaphysical bent and English audience. Far more remarkable is the detailed topographical knowledge the article displays. Roland Mathias has trod every route Henry Vaughan might have taken, frequently stopping to look, listen and record. The article is a labour of love.

Every time I stop my exile's way to look across from Penkelly or Cross Oak to Newton or pause above the unrivalled valley moving from Bwlch towards the ancient Vaughan home at Tretower Court, I feel the beauty of the scene hurt me, and I am conscious then, as perhaps at no other time, of the inadequacy of human emotions, hooped as they are by time and diversion.

The love of natural beauty here is very close to religious love. More than the artist's or the scientist's faithful recording of scenery is involved. There is a profound emotional response and a sense of man's inadequacy before Nature.

With the unfolding of Dock Leaves from number 1 in 1949 to number 22 in 1957, Roland set out his stall as a writer. He had already made a significant mark, but during this period, and in fifty-one published items, he emerged to a readership in Wales as a short-story writer of considerable skill and versatility, a poet of known achievement and still developing strength, and an extraordinarily gifted scholar and critic. The accomplishment is the more remarkable for being achieved in the midst of a demanding professional career and a busy and responsible social life.

In 1956 he published The Eleven Men of Eppynt and

OTHER STORIES, his only collection and almost his entire output in the genre. Perhaps he lacks the narrative inventiveness of the fiction-writer; more likely, he allowed himself less time than is needed to develop the story-telling art beyond the period that is demarcated by the publication of the volume. Nine of the fourteen stories are derived from his personal experience or scholarly interest in history. Most of the others, like the title story, are in the mould of the Anglo-Welsh short story; though different one from the other and distinctively his, they are yet familiar in their settings, themes and characters.

The earliest story, 'Take Hold on Hell', was first published in 1942 (under the title 'Study in Hate') in a little quarterly magazine called SEVEN. It is set in gaol and the main figure, a prisoner who is abject, sick and confused, pleads with a brutal warder to be allowed to see the governor, so that he can find someone at home in Wales with the influence to free him. The harsh refusal triggers an attack of blind fury that sends the warder over the rail of the landing, through a gap in the safety netting and on to the floor below. The background, fresh in the writer's memory, is drawn with vivid economy. The image of the *little grey squares high up in the dark that were his window* was also used in the poem 'Bars', and there is scope within the story for more detail of prison life, especially the sounds from neighbouring cells and the strange cries of the mentally disturbed.

Five of the stories appeared in DOCK LEAVES. In 'Block-System', Ben Davies, expatriate dairyman (a familiar enough figure in Welsh story) is the helpless victim of bureaucracy in wartime London. He rises above petty tyranny and his family's irritation and despair by recourse to an inner life that is his child-hood in Wales. 'The Palace', which appeared in number 2, is a well-dressed ghost story. It draws on Pembrokeshire landscape and history (the setting is Lamphey Palace, main seat of the Devereux family), although the central character has, like Roland Mathias himself, newly arrived from England. The other three stories are set in Wales and in their different ways bid fair to be considered archetypally Anglo-Welsh. 'The Eleven Men of Eppynt' was published in number 5, 1951. For it, the writer chose scenery very close to his proper home and familiar from his holidays in Breconshire. He adds to topo-graphical accuracy references to Welsh history and legend (Llewelyn Olaf, Ysbaddaden, Olwen, Arthur and Merlin), to the close-fistedness of Cardis, to country ways (*the iron crock of dough hidden in a raked cavity, roofed with wood and engreyed coals*), and frequent use of sentence structures and turns of phrase that imitate the Welsh language (*If there's no flour with you, then what are you going to do?*). The story, which may have had its inspiration in the bitter winter of 1947, is simple enough. After nine days cut off by snow in their mountain village, eleven men set out from Upper Chapel for Brecon to buy bread. The journey downhill to the town is hard, and once there the weak-willed succumb to the temptation of strong drink. Having bought the bread, they turn again to the mountain, but the familiar way is obliterated by darkness and snow. They struggle through a minor epic of difficulties and danger, guided at the last by the light gleaming across the white waste from the window in Matti's cottage. It is a story that could have been written a decade or two earlier, to stand alongside Geraint Goodwin's 'Janet Ifan's Donkey' perhaps, but it is more than pastiche. It is written with gusto and glitters like the lamplit snow with allusion and imagery.

The title 'Ffynnon Fawr' (number 10, 1953) is immediately recognizable to readers familiar with Roland's life, though presumably not to most subscribers to DOCK LEAVES. The setting is indeed the ruin of the farm where the writer was born and, like Rendel Morgan, the only character in this story, spent the first four and a half years of his life. There the parallel ends. Morgan has been given a mission by his dying mother, to return to Ffynnon Fawr, the home the family left to emigrate to Australia many years before. On a grey day of ceaseless rain Rendel seeks and finally finds the derelict house close to the edge of the man-made lake and, within it, a room that invites him to rest. There he sleeps and in a dream re-enactment of the past, hears his father's voice berating obstreperous neighbours, *senses stillness, and yet no peace*, and knows he is *too timid to make a future where the generations cried out to him in their sleep*. 'Ffynnon Fawr' is a story that is sparing of narration but heavy with atmospheric description – a melodrama.

In 'The Match' (number 20, 1956) the reader is on familiar Welsh ground again, for the story of frustrated love that unfolds in the mind of Wynford, the protagonist, of male friendship and rivalry and love lost, is set against the action of a school rugby match. The game is described with all the skill that, as a former player and coach, the writer could muster. The setting is Pembroke Dock, the rugby pitch below the school, and the teams and even key players are readily identifiable. Typically, the wider landscape is viewed in historic depth. The counterpoint of rugby action and the interior narrative is well sustained as Wynford is led by the example of schoolboy courage and determination to resolve his personal dilemma. The inner drama of relationships in this story hints at potential for a fresh line of development that was not to be realized.

A near-fatal accident he uses in 'Incident in Majorca' is recollected in the 'Mallorcan Notebook' he published in DOCK LEAVES number 21 –

It was twenty-five years since my temple was nicked by death in this gorge. A touch, the kiss that a hundredweight gives in falling.

In the story, it is the rather solitary, independent-minded boy Littlejohn who thus escapes death, while leading his reluctant pursuers on a tramp through the rocky Torrente del Paryes that is indeed fatal to one of the group, his stepfather, whom he despises. All the circumstances of the story are recalled from Roland's earliest visit to Majorca, as a member of a school party from Caterham. Whether Mallinson, the stepfather in the story, and the boys in the pursuing party are drawn from life is hard to say, but the baked landscape of the island is recalled with great clarity, and there is a little of the author himself in Littlejohn.

The greater part of 'The Rhine Tugs' is auto-biography. The small boy who watches from a high window the tugs busy on the Rhine, and knows each one by name and by the stripes on its funnel, is Roland at about six years of age. The skill of this re-creation of childhood leaves the reader regretting that its author did not give more of his time to his own story. To place the childhood incidents into a fictional framework, he invents a displaced person, curiously childlike in an overcoat *several sizes too big for his rather puny frame*. With the eyes of the child he once was and the memory of the city as he knew it, this alien watches on the cinema screen the newsreel image of the shattered remains of Cologne, until he can no longer bear to be the only one in the audience who is moved. He leaves the cinema and walks, eventually alongside a canal where the movement of the water and reflected light conjure up the memory of tugs on the river of his childhood city.

In 'The Rhine Tugs' Roland Mathias exploits the power of an exact memory, but more than that he conveys with great subtlety the sensibilities of a child, the perception of physical realities and human relationships. He uses the same remarkable skill in 'Incident in Majorca' and, from a different perspective, in 'Match' and 'Agger Makes Christmas'. The last named, like 'Incident in Majorca', owes a great deal to the author's own school-days. One of its strengths is the confident description of end of term at boarding-school, the boys packing their trunks and planning for Christmas. For Agger it will be the usual lonely affair, spent mostly at the school, because his father is overseas, ministering to the souls of Papuans. The portrayal of this boy is a notable success.

If he had an illusion, it was that he was something of a foil. Out of much girding might come warmth and a companionable spark . . . One could only be ready . . . Already he was withdrawing from the circle, practising for his future wounds.

If his Christmas too is to be different from the other

days of the year, and memorable, Agger has to make it so. The implementation of his plan is the climax of the story. It is unexpected and involves a measure of contrivance not uncharacteristic of the genre, especially given its thirties ambience. The story winds down with a closing description that encompasses its themes: Christmas, companionable warmth and domesticity, the regimented monotony of days and urban growth creeping over the countryside. The diction and dialogue of 'Agger Makes Christmas' are apt and the characterization is economical and exact. More than most stories in the volume it demonstrates Roland Mathias's potential as a writer of fiction.

School provides the setting of one other story, but not the kind of school the author had directly experienced (other than very briefly in his childhood). The schools in 'Cassie Thomas' are the mixed elementary schools in south Wales in the early 1940s. The time is significant, because the climax is precipitated by the arrival of evacuee children at the small country school where Cassie is headteacher. The story, however, is about her strangely divided self, the product of determination to break away from her home, where *her father sat in the kitchen in his shirt-sleeves, with the coal-dust deep under the rims of his nails*. She works hard at her education and through it finds a voice and an adopted persona that distinguishes her from the ordinary people of the mining valleys. Eventually she becomes a schoolteacher. The other person who shares her body is watched and admired, even by herself. As she gains more experience, it acquires greater permanence and control, but without entirely displacing the watchful, uncertain creature at the core. Confrontation with a ghastly, overgrown bully among the evacuee children causes the collapse of the controlling self. She is humiliated before the pupils and her colleagues. Worse, after this breakdown, returned to her parents' home, she finds that the part of her that knew the ropes has gone for good. 'Cassie Thomas' is a brief and powerful story. In it the author seems to be commenting on an affliction that in some personalities prevents two self-images from being brought together into focus. He sees it as not uncommon, especially among the first educated generation to arise from the working class, who have to discard the familiar *Silly, soft things . . . that were out of place in the life of an educated woman* and discipline themselves to a kind of alien austerity. If they are to succeed, it must be by creating *a dummy* self. *Like many of her friends* [Cassie] *had had to make her dummy carefully, because there was no one at home who could show her how. None of her family had ever been educated, you see . . .*

The narrative bones of a group of stories were given to him by members of his family: 'One Bell Tolling', 'A Night for the Curing', and 'Block-System' by various uncles, 'Ffynnon Fawr' by his father. 'A Night for the Curing' is set *on the moor by Y Gât*, that is, Rhos Llangeler, Carmarthenshire, not many miles from Rhydlewis and close to the spirit of that place. On this poor land the bounty of a slaughtered pig is shared with neighbours in the expectation that the giver will in turn receive. But Methusalem Morris is mean and shifty and the prospect of giving in the traditional way leaves him writhing with inner conflict:

He sagged and stiffened, circled and deployed, crooked his neck and reached bolt upright all in the space of one normal emotion.

Execration, anxiety and cunning followed each other over his face like shadows over the stubble. His eyes ran shallow and deep by turns.

He plots to cheat his neighbours by saying the carcass has been stolen, and finds the next morning that it has indeed. The wily butcher congratulates him on his fine acting. The story is not as unremittingly harsh as those of MY PEOPLE, and the humour not sardonic. Also it is more moral; deceit is repaid, and the deceiver loses.

'One Bell Tolling' is an exercise in the direction of the macabre, but with a gentle grip, that contains hints of a mysterious power residing still in aboriginal Welshness. Morgan Williams farms in the Vale, but he is true Welsh, from hills above the mining valleys. His hands are not gnarled with his labour but have *a crude, unfinished look . . . long and slivered, slipping without warning from skin to nail . . . like the rudimentary claws of a great bird.* He is delivering potatoes in an old van and has with him a labourer, Hedley, and his own young son. Hedley goes with the son to visit his Mamgu and finds himself in a curious, darkened house that seems barely half in this world. Out of the gloom first Uncle Jack, a long-boned man, sick and crippled, and then Mamgu herself materialize. When the old woman stertorously offers the boy a shilling, Hedley, whose anxiety has grown to panic, drags him out of the house and at last to the familiar street and the battered van. The story is highly wrought, encrusted with imagery and elliptical.

Elliptical story-telling and dialogue and the extensive use of imagery to create dramatic atmosphere are features also of 'The Neutral Shore', which is a historical adventure. It is about covert action against 'owlers', the gangs of men operating along the south-east coast of England in about 1690, who exported wool or sheep illegally to France. Four men meet in the upstairs room of a tavern to set a trap for the smugglers. Their conversation is as shadowy as the darkened room in which it takes place. The only lights are guttering candles and later, as they ride out, an uncertain moon, the winking signals from land and sea, and a lantern that shows a man killed from behind by sabre-cut. Throughout, the reader must work on scanty clues to complete the narrative.

'Digression into Miracle' is the retelling of a piece of local Welsh history somewhat earlier in the seventeenth century. It is 27 June 1647 and Thomas Bushell, an engineer of sorts, is searching unsuccessfully for silver in mines among the mountains above Aberystwyth. He knows that an earlier and far more successful prospector, Hugh Middleton, has left great riches at the bottom of a deep, drowned shaft. The story focuses on four miners resting and smoking near the mouth of the adit they have been driving into the hillside above Talybont. Each is identified by name and by the dialect he uses as they complain about the work and speculate on the poisoning of the land and the waters in the locality. The climax comes swiftly as the pent-up water in Middleton's shaft bursts out of the hillside above them and floods down the slope to the village below. When the waters subside, they take their candles and enter the adit. In the explosion that follows one is killed. The story ends with a letter to Bushell from the Reverend Thomas Broadway congratulating him on his success: *Behold, sir, how deare you are to providence, which, for your sake hath vouchsafed to digresse into a miracle.*

'The Neutral Shore' and 'Digression into Miracle' were born of Roland's skill as a historian. They differ in their manner of telling, but have impressive strengths in the creation of atmosphere and a convincing re-creation of the past that is as accurate as scholarship can make it. (In his reviews of fiction, he is critical of abuse of history and would not follow that path himself.) Although the evidence is not great in amount, it is substantial in quality that, had he been minded, Roland Mathias might have bid fair to be a historical novelist of note.

With the publication of THE ELEVEN MEN OF EPPYNT, his excursions in the short story virtually ended. For all his facility in prose, he was not a prolific short-story writer, needing a particular stimulus or, more often, a given narrative as a starting-point. That is why, although they have certain common qualities (they are rich in imagery, particularly of landscape, and duality in character is a recurring theme), the stories do not bear the impress of a consistent style. Rather, each has its own style. Their quality is unquestionable, however, and was readily recognized by editors like John Lehmann (PENGUIN NEW WRITING) and J. Middleton Murry (THE ADELPHI). Among the handful of uncollected stories are a few from the 1940s and two, 'The Only Road Open' (ANGLO-WELSH REVIEW, No. 34, Winter 1964–5) and 'Siâms' (AWR, No. 64, Spring 1973), that are 'family' stories. In the latter, the narrator visits Aaron, an aged relative who is anxious that he should also visit Siâms, the only other survivor of his generation, to tell him how he (Aaron) has failed to carry on the family line. The story contrasts the portraits of the old men with their hopeful younger selves, *well-scrubbed . . . ascetic in their country boots . . . with an inbred suspicion of the world outside*. Sex is their undoing. The dissatisfaction and loss of ambition that come between are rooted in failure in relations with women, a product of their unworldliness.

In 'The Only Road Open', Alun is leaving his childhood home by bus in the middle of a snowy winter. He is desolate and wants to stop and go back, but with the memory of his father's funeral the previous July, he realizes that he has nothing to return to: he is already outside *the secret centre of being . . . and rapidly moving away*. The Glyn Collwn of this story, the graveyard and the funeral are the realities of Roland Mathias's birthplace and his father's final journey. The portrait of *the young dark italianate face . . . the streets of Llanelly etched in behind . . . the tricky, tireless out-half, tasselled cap on one finger; the veteran student, still young but bulging learnedly over his butterfly collar* is that of Evan Mathias. Although it is never safe to presume too far the truth to life of a piece of fiction, there is a significant part of the writer himself, presented with the characteristic element of duality in Alun, who sees

That other self of mine, that man I am but for age . . . up there, caught . . . when they sprinkled earth on his coffin I never knew it . . . But now I know it. I am there and here, trapped and yet free, if free only to ride away. There are two of me, and one of us must die.

III

Roland Mathias brought to the role of headteacher the same energy and commitment he had shown as a teacher: he led by inspiration and example. From Caterham and the schools where he had taught, with their cultural and sporting traditions, he brought to Pembroke Dock a strong enthusiasm for extra-curricular activities. He began or revived the school magazine, debating, drama and the Urdd, and encouraged a broad interest in the arts. Remarkably for the time and the south Pembrokeshire location, he introduced Welsh into the curriculum.

In December 1948, at the end of his first term, the local press was congratulating the school on its production of Shaw's ST JOAN in which the head and other members of staff had performed alongside pupils. The following year saw the production of Sheridan's SCHOOL FOR SCANDAL, and in 1950 Eliot's MURDER IN THE CATHEDRAL, in which the headteacher played the archbishop. All three were ambitious choices, even for a mixed cast of pupils and teachers, and all three, but particularly the last, were acclaimed locally as successes. An anonymous correspondent to the WEST WALES GUARDIAN criticized the involvement of staff in the play in a way that aroused the combative instincts of the head. His response in the school magazine THE PENFRO contains some of his guiding principles as an educationalist:

A school is a community or should be. The last thing we should seek to underline is that there is one set of people in it who make the rest do things and another set who have to do them. A community should be one, and every opportunity should be taken by teachers of crossing that usually necessary, but at all times limiting, line to work with, and take discipline from one another . . . There can be no finer training for community than the shelving of status for a common aim . . . Who says success is not important? Of course it is . . . for the enjoyment, education, future confidence and prowess of all who participate.

In April 1952 the school produced another verse play, VENUS OBSERVED by Christopher Fry, only two years after it had first appeared in the West End. This was one measure of Roland Mathias's determination to set high standards. Within three years of his taking up the post he was being referred to in the local press as *the esteemed* or *the distinguished* headmaster of the grammar school.

The scrap-book of this period reveals a life of extraordinary busyness for him and Molly, who was at the time caring for three young children, the third having been born in Pembroke Dock in March 1951. Molly became a pillar of the Women's Institute and they were both active in chapel affairs. He preached occasionally and was president of the United Evangelical Churches' Choral Festival and the Congregational Sunday School Anniversary. As well as acting in school plays, he performed leading roles for the Pembroke Arts Club drama society. In 1951, to mark the Festival of Britain, he arranged through the Arts Club an impressive exhibition of paintings, books and rare maps at the school. In the same year he became chairman of the Arts Club and of the Festival Year Athletic Sports. He regularly acted as adjudicator of literary and elocution events at several eisteddfodau in the neighbourhood. In his holidays he took on summer-school lecturing for the Workers' Educational Association and the British Council.

There was no remission of his work in education with the passing years and there was increasing responsibility outside school. He contributed *an acutely penetrating study of the working out of Christian values in a co-educational grammar school* (said the TIMES EDUCATIONAL SUPPLEMENT) to a book on THE SCHOOL AS A CHRISTIAN COMMUNITY, and in 1955 was appointed to the Central Advisory Council for Education in Wales. In the same year his school was redesignated a grammar-technical with an agricultural specialism and moved to new premises at Bush with a 100-acre site that included thirty-seven acres of farmland and twenty-nine acres of forestry. He wrote in educational journals about this experiment in secondary schooling. He promoted annual international youth meetings at the school premises in Pembroke Dock and later at Bush.

Each year at the school's prize-giving he spoke to the audience on a major issue. In December 1957 he answered critics of his regime who claimed that the school had expectations beyond the reach of pupils and pushed them into too many activities. In his response he defended an educational principle that was entirely in keeping with his personal philosophy and lifestyle:

It is the failure of intelligent pupils to apply their intelligence wisely, with a purposeful curiosity, that I find distressing. Failure to see that they waste hours every day, not in group activities but in unimaginative behaviour and unconstructive talk, both at home and in school. Hardly ever, in my experience, is academic failure related to over-dedication to other school activities: it is far more closely related to under-dedication to any sort of activity.

In March 1958, the WESTERN MAIL reported that Roland Mathias had been appointed to the headship of the Herbert Strutt School, Belper, Derbyshire. He remained at Pembroke Dock until the end of the summer term, in part at least to see to fruition the Festival of Wales Pageant, which he had written to commemorate the birth of Henry VII at Pembroke in 1457.

Through the summer term he and Molly were the special guests of numerous clubs and societies that wanted to express gratitude and wish them well. As the WEST WALES GUARDIAN commented, they had closely identified themselves with the social and religious life of the borough. On 1 August the pageant's cast of 500 assembled in heavy rain but the clouds lifted and, as the author had planned, the people of Pembroke re-enacted in the castle a piece of history with long Anglo-Welsh reverberations.

Belper is in the south of Derbyshire; Lawrence's Eastwood is not a dozen miles to the east in neighbouring Nottinghamshire. In 1958, it had only a few thousand more inhabitants than Pembroke Dock, but it was a good deal busier than the town that the Mathias family had left. Belper owed its character to the Industrial Revolution. Oil and paint industries had been added to the iron-founding and the textiles and hosiery manufacturing that had their roots in the eighteenth century. It was a fairly prosperous town and in George Herbert Strutt, a mill-owner, it had an outstanding benefactor with a sense of duty to his community. In 1909 he had founded and entirely funded the construction of the grammar school that bore his name. In the year before its jubilee, it had 600 pupils and well-established traditions including an annual 'Founder's Day' celebration, a Latin Declamations competition, a handsomely produced school magazine and a combined cadet force with Army and RAF sections.

The new headmaster was soon involved in the school's many extra-curricular activities. As at Pembroke Dock, he introduced rugby football and supported it, though now from the touch-line; again, he performed in a school play. He organized the 1959 Jubilee celebrations, instigated the construction of a pavilion on the playing fields, enhanced the opportunities of pupils to pursue the subjects that interested them and the university prospects of sixth-formers. His commitment to the education of the whole person and to the concept of the school as a community with shared moral and intellectual values was pursued energetically but never with solemn earnestness. The pupils at Herbert Strutt School remembered him for his sense of humour and his jokes as much as for his enthusiasm to lead and to raise expectations.

Had he been preoccupied only with the multifarious demands of school life, the achievement in Belper would have been substantial. The expectations of service to the community that he set for himself and others, however, made calls that extended beyond the working day. In a Founder's Day speech he took parents and pupils to task on this matter of principle:

it has saddened me not a little to encounter [pupils] . . . who have been allowed to grow up talking about their rights and not at all about their duties . . . we should begin to teach the younger generation the essential values . . . Christian and humanist can join in this . . . it is the only way we shall deserve to survive.

As at Pembroke Dock he kept up a busy round of out-of-school engagements. He had been elected to the Board of Governors of Nottingham University before his arrival in Belper and was frequently called upon to give talks on educational issues. He was soon a leading figure in the local music society and spoke to the Derby Poetry Society on Henry Vaughan. The Congregational church was the centre of one sphere of activity for the family, and his reputation as a preacher took him to other churches. Nor was that all. He journeyed back to Wales on occasion to lecture and broadcast about literature on the Welsh Home Service, and in 1961, following Raymond Garlick's departure to take up a teaching post in the Netherlands, he began his long and dedicated labour as editor of THE ANGLO-WELSH REVIEW.

The only respite in this period was brought about by his election to a Schoolmasters' Studentship at Balliol College which enabled him to spend the whole of the Hilary Term 1961 at Oxford. There he concluded research on which he had been intermittently engaged for almost twenty years. It concerned a minor uprising among Catholic recusants in Archenfield, that part of Herefordshire close to the Monmouthshire border, at Whitsun in 1605, the same year as the Gunpowder Plot. The reason for the disturbances, which lasted about six weeks, the instigators, the identity of a certain William Morgan, and the way in which the law finally prevailed are the ingredients of a tale of detection painstakingly unravelled in WHITSUN RIOT, published in 1963. In the book the documentary evidence of an event that had previously merited only a footnote in history is examined in minute detail, and the villages and lanes of Archenfield, surprisingly little changed since the seventeenth century, were explored with similar care.

This border land, its topography and the major figures in its history have remained one of the most potent sources of inspiration for Roland Mathias. That the Devereux family, to which the earl of Essex belonged, had its roots in Archenfield; that Sir Gelly Meyrick was one of the Essex faction in 1601 and was executed with him; that there was bitter rivalry between the Devereux family and the Cecils (in which the latter ultimately triumphed); and that their feud was fought out locally by their followers, Paul Delahay of Allt-yr-ynys in Waterstone, steward of the Cecil lands in Monmouthshire, and John Arnold (or Arnalt as he is known in texts of the period) of Llanthony, are all material to a full understanding of several later poems.

The ancient quarrel and its curiously mingled religious, political and materialistic aspects drew the historian and the poet. Finding the Devereux connection strong in Pembrokeshire must have reinforced his interest, but perhaps above all it was the place that fascinated him. He has walked the hills and levels, marked the scattered hamlets and farms, the brooks and woods, and knows that, before it was Archenfield, this was the old Welsh region of Ergyng. The March, the border between England and Wales, the shifting border between English and Welsh, is more to him than an intellectual preoccupation. It reflects his perception of his own position, on the edge of things, viewing them with engrossed detachment.

WHITSUN RIOT was widely and, for the most part, favourably reviewed. As well as being an absorbing exercise in detection, with an unexpected hero in the Welsh-speaking earl of Worcester, who contrived to still the commotion without bloodshed, the book is a stylistic *tour de force*. Twenty-five years were to pass before Roland Mathias returned to historical research to write the chapters on the Civil War and its aftermath for the PEMBROKESHIRE COUNTY HISTORY (VOL. III), and more importantly to explore again the borderland of Wales and England in his pursuit of the Silurist, Henry Vaughan. Through the intervening years, poetry's gain was history's loss – though not entirely, because in his indefatigably scrupulous approach to reviewing new books on the history of Wales, we see, again and again, the scholar obsessed with his subject.

His commitment to Wales, incompletely self-acknowledged at Pembroke Dock (although he offended some locals by flying the Red Dragon above the school on St David's Day – a nationalist gesture in their eyes) grew plainer in his renewed exile. The ties, particularly with Breconshire, were strong, more so since his parents had settled in the town of Brecon in 1940. Regularly at holidays he travelled south from Derbyshire to see them. His relationship with his mother was as close as ever, but they had little now in common. As he had made his way in education and literature, she had become increasingly detached from the world and eccentric in her own brand of puritanism. Evan Mathias, on the other hand, no longer in robust health, and mellower, was proud of his son's achievements and eager to discuss shared intellectual interests with him. At about this time, Roland Mathias described in an essay, 'The Border', how he is instinctively moved at that moment in his journey when he crosses into or out of Wales:

If I halt momentarily on the western edge of Brown Clee and call it blessed, is it not simple distance that holds me, the tract of mist and recollection floating out like a horizon behind the Ludlow Hills? Years and years ago my father halted on the top of Birdlip, with the same pain in his heart, and said to us children, 'Let's go back!' 'Yes, yes,' we chorused, all except my mother, who said faintly, 'Don't be silly. You know you can't.' 'No, we can't. But let's look back anyway,' rejoined my father sternly. And so we did . . . But if ever the entry to the Forest of Dean looked like the beginning of a ride that cut bareback home, it did then. It was the edge of being, the border of the land of the lifting heart . . . Three or four times a year at least for almost as long as I can remember, I have come by one of the roads that mounts imperceptibly from the Herefordshire plain to the point where the Wye . . . emerges from the hills . . . I murmured to myself, long before the border was officially marked, 'This is it'. And felt the change in me, felt it in the spine . . . Sometimes I school myself to forget it . . . But the plan never succeeds. Spine and tongue will not let it, if will the eye.

Elsewhere in the same essay, he imagines himself somehow prevented at the boundary – *That will be the fate, I am sure, of one who has counted himself out and in so many times . . . And all I can do will be to look sadly over the wall of Wales like an earth-weary Adam into his next-door Eden.*

On one of the many return journeys, for the October half-term holiday in 1960, he arrived in Brecon to find that his father had suffered a stroke earlier in the day and was partially paralysed. For a time,

Evan Mathias retained a strong hold on life, but in July 1962 he died and was interred in the graveyard of the little chapel on the hillside above Aber, where his wife's parents were buried.

Roland was still fairly new to Belper when THE FLOODED VALLEY appeared in 1960. Putnam, his London publisher, advertised it as his first collection of verse. It was his fourth, though twenty-five of the thirty-three poems, including the title poem, had already been collected in THE ROSES OF TRETOWER. After the spate of poetry leading up to the publication of that book, the eight new items are a small crop to represent the years 1952–60.

'Scithwen Valley' is a revised version of 'Scithon Valley' which appeared in DOCK LEAVES in 1955, where in its final stanza it had clear echoes of Gerard Manley Hopkins. He first wrote the poem simply to celebrate landscape, the heat of the day, the sun *bantam brown* reflected in the scummy water of a tank, lambs, kestrels (*Tweedy hangers about that the wild/Sun misses*), a distant tractor, heard but not seen, all fixed in that moment by the poet's perceptions and art:

> My lambs, my chugaway
> In the valley, kestrels bitter for food,
> Mine in this halt to gather and grass in sun for good!

In the original, the sunlit day, the lambs and man's toil on the land were enough to outweigh the slimed water, the birds of prey and a barren field above. The revision reconstructs the occasion, tilting the balance arm the other way and imposing on the same impressions a mood of bitter self-analysis:

What other man, away
In a bantam past, bit out a tongue and stood
Shamed and sick on his hillock when the sun was good?

'Orielton Empty' describes the neglected mansion and park of Orielton, seat of the Owen family that played a major part in Pembrokeshire life from the seventeenth century until the twentieth. In his short story 'The Palace' the writer draws on the history of a rival clan, the Devereux, and its ancient seat at Lamphey. He has the historian's preoccupation with time and age, and in his years at Pembroke Dock dug deep into local landscape and genealogy. The story, this poem and others bear out his assertions in a review of a novel by Llewelyn Powys (in DOCK LEAVES) *for me, place, the traditional and ancestral associations of place are enormously important.*

Of the other newer poems, 'Marston Sicca' and 'Conversation on Stackpole Head' also remind the reader that the historian, the actor and the poet are one in Roland Mathias. He can adopt with every appearance of ease a mode of utterance that seems to belong to the seventeenth century in diction and word order, and to the stage. The same skills, allied to his response to place, are apparent in 'Cascob', an exercise in the creation of an atmosphere of menace. The finest of the additions is very different in character. 'For Warren Davies, Two Years Dead' is an elegy to a Pembroke friend that plainly records his life, his manner of speaking and the truth that he spoke. The poet as *remembrancer* brings the whole man before us in celebration and mourning.

. . . this week the clematis
With which you set our hill court in purple

67

Twice is page again, and up to the lattice
Creeps. How slip, how preening cast of yours, can it recouple
This switch of land to you and greenly in it
Grapple your ailing hand?

It was cold,
Cold of a Sunday morning early in Church Street
When you turned in your sleep, and old
Morning, at last unmanned, curtained his gold.

Putnam's imprint and connections secured for the book reviews in the quality press. THE TIMES LITERARY SUPPLEMENT remarked the attractiveness of *the exact imagist portrayal of Welsh town and country scenes* and, in the best poems, the poet's *taciturn, rather stoically unhappy references to himself.* Elizabeth Jennings, writing in the GUARDIAN, thought the book *forceful and disturbing. Mr Mathias,* she wrote, *looks at landscapes and sees not a tranquil collection of forms but a gathering of diverse energies.* In the OBSERVER, Al Alvarez found it *an uneven book,* in which landscape is made *odd and upsetting by the eye of the beholder, yet also upset by his fragmentary rhetoric.* Though troubled by the obscurity of some, Glyn Jones in THE ANGLO-WELSH REVIEW (No. 26) wrote of the *assurance and accomplishment* of the poems, and granted that the poet had the *mastery of whatever language he wishes to use.*

Roland spent six years in Belper. In September 1964, he took up the headship of King Edward VI Five Ways, Birmingham, a boys' grammar school of ancient foundation and considerable distinction, which, since 1958, had been housed in new premises in the suburb of Bartley Green. It had some 600 pupils, a plethora of clubs and societies, again including a combined cadet force, and a notable rugby union tradition. On his arrival, he supplied the school magazine with a mock 'Who's Who' entry that listed the schools where he had taught, with the observation *Does not yet despair of the human race*, and declared among his interests rugby football, hockey, drama and choral singing *all past the positively last date of personal performance, now supplemented by Creative Writing, Historical Research and Gardening*.

The school had a stable staff and clear educational goals. The sixth form was more than a hundred strong and the great majority of sixth-formers proceeded to university. The new head taught Latin to first-formers and put an experienced, steady hand to the tiller. In 1966–7 he was elected to a second schoolmaster fellowship. It took him for the spring term 1967, *by luck and high tide*, to the department of English at University College, Swansea. There he found himself, rather uneasily at first, in the company of Vernon Watkins, who was halfway through his tenure of a Gulbenkian Fellowship in Poetry in the same department. He describes their time together there in the chapter he contributed to the memorial volume, VERNON WATKINS 1906–1967, edited by Leslie Norris (1970).

At Five Ways he was less conspicuously involved in the extra-curricular activities of the school than he had been in his previous posts, but he worked assiduously behind the scenes with a generous parents' association to extend and improve the premises and facilities. The change was in part a product of age and experience, and in part a consequence of the increasing demands of literature, demands which were now formally recognized: in 1968 he received a Welsh Arts Council award for services to writing in

Wales. In the summer of 1969 Roland retired from headmastering. He and Molly moved to a bungalow in Brecon, only a few hundred yards from the substantial house where his mother, in her late seventies now, and sturdily independent, lived alone. They visited her daily and her death in 1979 left a large gap in their lives.

IV

With the support of a Welsh Arts Council bursary, Roland embarked upon his second career as a full-time writer. A great deal of his time was devoted to THE ANGLO-WELSH REVIEW. When he took over the editorship with No. 27 in 1960, he wanted to create a complete spectrum of Welsh interests in English, not in literature alone, but in all the humanities, because he felt it was something that had not previously been realized in the minds of English-speakers in Wales. It was a political agenda, because he believes that literature is not created in a vacuum, and it expressed the educationalist's will to inform and raise the aspirations of others. As there was no ready-made Anglo-Welsh literary tradition, he sought to identify and draw together the relevant strands – in effect, to create one. The wide range of interests is a reflection of his own catholic tastes. He strove to build up the magazine in terms of its contacts and contributors so that it would become known within and outside the literary field as a symbol of unity of interest. Viewed now with hindsight, AWR is a monument to Roland Mathias, his prodigious energy and versatility, his acumen and skill as editor, his unflagging patience and zeal in the task he had set himself. The magazine absorbed a great deal of his intellectual energy and contains a large part of his literary output. It was a personal platform, but also a work of service and self-abnegation.

One indication of his editorial approach is the richness of the contents of almost any individual number. AWR normally contained poems, short stories and articles. Though articles on literature predominated, there were frequently others on aspects of language, theatre, music, history, the plastic arts, topography and politics. Contributors were mostly Welsh, or of Welsh origins or affiliations, but many were of other cultures and backgrounds. A few were still in school, others had been born in the early years of the century. They came from the cities and counties of England, from Scotland and the Republic of Ireland, from France, Germany, Russia and Yugoslavia; numerous states of the USA were represented, along with Canada, South Africa, India and countries in South America.

As editor, Roland was always generous in his praise of those who supported and sustained the magazine through many threats and vicissitudes, especially Raymond Garlick and the band of faithful helpers in Pembroke Dock, and H. G. Walters and Sons, the Tenby printers. Although the number of subscribers gradually increased, there were never enough to make AWR viable. In 1959, it received its first Arts Council grant but no promise of future security, and in the editorial to No. 29 its imminent demise was announced. In No. 31, however, the editor offered belated thanks for further grant aid, and in No. 41 he wrote that the body that was by that time the Welsh Arts Council had, by providing some guarantee of continuity and sufficient funding to pay contributors, helped to improve the standard of the magazine. In No. 50, while giving credit to the Welsh Arts Council for its ten years of support, he observed that the diminution in the grant was putting all at risk. Against this background of insecurity, especially in the early years of his editorship, and neglect of

Anglo-Welsh literature, he moulded the magazine into a comprehensive expression of the culture of English-speaking Wales and a bridge with Welsh-speaking Wales.

The identity of the magazine was developed in editorials that are as thought-provoking as they are entertaining. Most are of considerable length. They deal with controversies in contemporary Welsh life as well as with literary topics. They include tributes to recently dead writers, such as John Cowper Powys, T. Harri Jones, Vernon Watkins, Cyril Hodges, B. L. Coombes and David Jones, and two who wrote in Welsh, D. J. Williams and Waldo Williams. Several of these obituaries emphasize the quality of the man as much as the skill of the writer. For the two last named, Roland felt a special affinity. Waldo Williams was a Quaker and a pacifist who had suffered prison for his convictions. D. J. Williams, also a committed Christian, is remembered for his cheerfulness and humanity, his simplicity, generosity and dedication to the nationalist cause, and because, unlike many contemporary Welsh-language writers, *he stretched out a friendly hand to the Welsh who had lost their language.*

The building of bridges between the literatures of Wales and enhancing the status of that in English are recurring themes. In developing them, he recognizes the importance of the establishment of an English section of Yr Academi Gymreig (the Welsh Academy), in which he had played an important part, of the Literature Department of the Welsh Arts Council and of the launch of the Writers of Wales series and new magazines – POETRY WALES, MABON and PLANET. More frequently, he laments the failure of schools and colleges, and especially the University of Wales, to study Anglo-Welsh writing, as some universities in France and North America already did. He admonishes the popular media, and those in Wales professionally equipped to do so, for not stimulating interest in Anglo-Welsh literature or providing the essential oxygen of review and critical appraisal, and deprecates *the London blackout*, that metropolitan neglect of writing from Wales, unless it has found recognition via the United States. In a quarter of his editorials Roland Mathias wrote on these issues, from time to time recording modest and local progress, but more frequently registering only gloom.

He worked to win more attention for Anglo-Welsh writing because of his confidence in its literary worth, because he found in it evidence of more humanity than appeared elsewhere in contemporary letters, and because it was Welsh and its support therefore part of his mission. In his editorial to No. 30 he challenged the basis upon which Alvarez had made his selection of NEW POETRY for Penguin and the argument in the introduction to the anthology that there is no place for gentility in the poetry of a century that has seen two world wars, the holocaust and the threat of nuclear destruction. *It seems a pity*, he writes, *that no Christian, no continuing humanist for that matter, can readily be recognised as a poet*. Roland Mathias's moral stance is clear and consistent: writing is not therapy, not a pumping-out of *society's sewage* for the writer's own sake. In the same editorial he applauds the selection of D. J. Williams's HEN DŶ FFERM as the representative Welsh text in the collection of the Council of Europe. The contrast with NEW POETRY could hardly be greater, for *D. J. . . . has loved Wales and her language as few have loved them, shirking neither calumny nor imprisonment. What he has had to say has always been simple and ennobling . . .*

Wales and the Welsh language constitute another recurring theme. The discussion is opened in his first editorial in the course of a perceptive appraisal of Raymond Williams's BORDER COUNTRY, and pursued in No. 29 in remarks about political developments, mostly in connection with a new policy for water conservation which shows that, since Tryweryn, government had been more sensitive to local communities. This hardly mitigates the affront he feels at the existence in 1962 of a ministerial portfolio for 'housing, local government and Welsh affairs'. But the blame lay in part close to home: *Wales can be recognised as equal and different just as soon as Welshmen en masse see themselves that way. And isn't it time?* He rejects the call for a bilingual National Eisteddfod, saying that he expects monoglot English-speaking readers of the magazine to support the concept of equal validity for Welsh, and to want to protect the culture of the Eisteddfod from infiltration by English. He counters the anti-nationalist views expressed in the BBC Wales Radio Lecture in 1973, saying that Wales could not continue to be distinct and different from its neighbours if Welsh became extinct. Furthermore, he argues, whereas Wales has a valid native culture in Welsh, with the exception of a small number of talented but ill-supported Anglo-Welsh writers, it has only *a deprived and feeble English regional culture in English.*

This beacon of Welshness lit the sky first from his home in Coxbench, near Derby, in 1964 from Inkberrow in Worcestershire and, following his last move in 1969, from the house in Brecon that was already by a strange fate named Deffrobani, after the summer country whence (Iolo Morganwg said) the Welsh had originally come to Britain. During this period he made himself an outstanding expert in Celtic studies and early Welsh history. This too appears in editorials that consider the legitimacy of the story of Madoc and the Welsh Indians of North America, and Arthurian legend.

Far more evidence of the scope of Roland's scholarship is to be found in the extraordinary range of his reviewing. For THE ANGLO-WELSH REVIEW he wrote 124 reviews in which he deals in considerable detail with more than 160 substantial books. In addition to full-length reviews, many of which have the dimensions and critical substance of articles, he frequently contributed brief notes on other magazines, tracts, pamphlets and spoken-word recordings. Although treated more briefly, even the latter were never dismissed cursorily. The bulk of his work was undertaken during the period of his own editorship, but he was also a reviewer while Raymond Garlick and, later, Gillian Clarke were at the helm. He occasionally reviewed with the same painstaking care for other magazines such as POETRY WALES, and on a regular basis in the 1980s for BRITISH BOOK NEWS and NINNAU ('The North American Welsh Newsletter'). It is characteristic of the man that on occasions when he reviewed for these journals a book he had already reviewed for AWR, the text was entirely different, not a recycling of what he had written previously. Multiple drafts of reviews show how much they were changed in the making. Roland Mathias is incapable of unconsidered judgements and facile journalism.

The scope of interests and erudition displayed in the reviews is very wide. For AWR he tackled poetry, novels and literary criticism, especially, but not exclusively, work by or about Anglo-Welsh writers. Among those whose new writing he reviewed at every opportunity were Dannie Abse, Emyr Humphreys, David Jones and John Cowper Powys, but the range includes every Anglo-Welsh writer of significance. He regularly reviewed topographical books, principally those concerned with Wales, occasionally biography and autobiography, and French texts, particularly those about the Breton language and culture. History is the largest category. He reviewed seventy-six history books, the great majority works by academics – about Welsh historical figures such as John Dee, David Samwell and Howel Harris; Welsh Nonconformity and recusancy; Welsh rural and industrial life; and above all, the uncertain zone of early Wales and the Celts in Britain and Europe.

As a reviewer of poetry and fiction, he declared early his focus upon what appears on the page and not the writer's psychology. He applied sure and reasoned standards to the themes and techniques of all his major contemporaries. In the literature of the 1960s and 1970s he searched for, and rarely found, *dignity and good sense*, while *egoism of the nastiest, most boring and self-exculpatory kind* [was] *all too common*. Reviews gave him the opportunity to express his discontent with the spirit of the age, sometimes by drawing a contrast between the writer's work and society; thus he commends Emyr Humphreys for his *infallible ear for conversation* which re-creates life as it was *before the yowling of the sixties and seventies began*. Writers who, he argues, are not more sensitive than their fellow men but gifted with the ability to communicate their feelings have a responsibility to humanity to select their subjects wisely. He praises the skill Rhys Davies employs in telling a sordid tale but asks, *Why choose to write about this*? He remarks the irony that young poets in Britain and America lament the extinction of individuality in mass culture while embracing an internationalism in poetry which . . . *promotes just that disappearance of valid societies . . . which it affects to regret.* He sees poets *trapped by political and sociological factors* and concludes *it's already happening here to those who haven't grown up into some sort of wisdom.*

If he was disturbed by the manifestations of an age of subverted moral values and blurred distinctions, there were still poets to celebrate, such as Raymond Garlick, for his unfailing *verbal mastery and historic perception*, and John Tripp, the variety of whose approaches to the nationalist theme is remarked as well as his *constant 'fizz' of phrase.* As a body of work, the reviews of literature reaffirm long-standing interests and give regular reminders of the extraordinary breadth and detail of his reading, such as his familiarity with the poetry of William Morris and Anthony Powell's fiction, his enthusiasm for the work of Ivor Gurney and David Jones, and his obsession with Hopkins as man and poet.

The reviews of history reveal him as a champion of Welsh Nonconformity. He rejects sociological treatises on the decline of the chapel and looks for that rounded view of Dissent in which its achievements are presented without apology. He continually urges further discussion of Nonconformist democracy and recognition of the debt owed to Howel Harris and his followers for the rediscovery of Wales's self-respect. He found in documents of the period like THE DIARY OF THOMAS JENKINS OF LLANDEILO, 1826–1870, evidence that the stereotype of a rigid and tyrannical chapel society is a falsehood perpetrated by the writers of the twentieth century, *romantic egoists in most cases*, who slander the past to justify themselves. This view, so distant from the orthodoxy of Anglo-Welsh literary opinion, is largely derived from his sense of rootedness in that hard rural environment from which his father's father had sprung, that was so close in time and place to Caradoc Evans's Rhydlewis but had left so different a mark. Reviewing a book on the agricultural community in south-west Wales at the turn of the century, he thinks it *almost incredible that our grandfathers . . . lived so differently*.

Dealing with books on Thomas Jones, the artist of Pencerrig, or John Owen, vice-chancellor of Oxford University in the time of Cromwell, Roland has the same scholarly approach that displays almost casually his extensive knowledge of the periods concerned and of Welsh connections. It is doubtful whether specialist journals routinely gave more attention to studies of the history of Wales than AWR during the period of his editorship. He writes sympathetically and with insight on THE CALENDAR OF ANCIENT PETITIONS RELATING TO WALES, commenting, *It is another world, and yet one that ancestry keeps beating in the heart*. He detects numerous errors and omissions in a book on Michael Faraday in Wales, reexamines data in a treatise on rural migration in the Marches to show that the author has come to incomplete and faulty conclusions, and adds another dimension to research on the Society for the Propagation of the Gospel by referring to its work in America.

Although he gives warm praise where it is merited, few books on Celtic studies and the early history of Wales entirely escape censure. Some amateurs who enter the lists are roundly trounced for inaccuracies and professionals have their theories examined and, occasionally, rejected – for proposing a Pictish dynasty in Gwynedd, or a view of travel by sea that is at variance with the findings of Continental experts and carbon 14 dating, or a plan of Iron Age houses that conflicts with his own observation.

Some of his most interesting work is in the shadowy realm where proto-history meets pseudo-history, in books on Arthur and Madoc. The latter he found especially absorbing. MADOC AND THE DISCOVERY OF AMERICA by Richard Deacon, which he reviewed in No. 38 (Winter 1967), and found ill-written, badly organized and occasionally misinformed, is the principal source of his long poem 'Madoc'. In this and other reviews on the same theme he held to his belief in the Welsh discovery of America and the Welsh Indians against the scepticism of professional historians. In the review of Deacon's book, he concludes that if America was named after a Bristolian, Richard Amerycke, and not Amerigo Vespucci, then it is named Welshly – the continent of Ap Meurig.

In his reviews Roland exploited a formidable and eclectic scholarship, much of it gathered from first-hand acquaintance with relevant documents or, in the case of topographical books, from having walked the routes described. It is his habit to *handle and use* books, hence his punctiliousness over accuracy and the aptness of maps and illustrations and their proximity to the relevant textual reference. He has the keenest of eyes for solecisms, spelling errors, inconsistencies in footnotes and editorial lapses of all kinds. His last review for AWR was in No. 81, 1985; no one has adequately replaced him.

He also published a few articles in AWR that are closely allied to his reviews. Nos. 36 and 38 have extended evaluations of the poetry of Dannie Abse, whom he considers *one of the most satisfying and genuine of contemporary poets*. This does not mean wholehearted endorsement of Abse's output. Indebtedness to Dylan Thomas in the early poems has *excruciating results*, and he finds poems that are bad or indifferent because of their obscurity. He nevertheless responds to Abse's belief in *the power of human love, in the faithfulness of good as well as evil's insidiousness, and the possible validity of religious experience*. The study of Alun Lewis in No. 67 gives due prominence to the influence on his writing of war, sexuality and the shock of India, but it is, he finds, Lewis's tenacious idealism and his concept of personal and universal love that distinguish him. The theme of Emyr Humphreys's *puritan seriousness about the purpose of living* had preoccupied Roland since first reading HEAR AND FORGIVE in 1953. In an article in No. 70 he focuses particularly on OUTSIDE THE HOUSE OF BAAL, which he considers outstanding. It is the depiction of religion, in this case J. T. Miles's Calvinistic Methodism, in Welsh society that draws him as a critic.

Yr Hen Gorff was the very symbol of that Wales from which the English language, together with the anglicised gentry, and all their hangers-on had been shut out, that Wales which had organised itself on egalitarian principles and amongst whose values the pursuit of wealth and social standing made scarcely a mark.

He sees constantly posed in Emyr Humphreys's

novels *the enormous question of whether we know and understand what good is.*

There is more to editing than selecting the content of a magazine: Roland took unusual pains in corresponding with contributors, prompting some to undertake research for which he himself could not find the time, and he planned the development of the magazine. There were several editorial coups, such as the collection of personal and critical tributes to Vernon Watkins in No. 39, and the Geraint Goodwin–Edward Garnett correspondence in Nos. 49 and 50. Perhaps the most important was the publication, also in No. 50 of a new poem by David Jones, 'The Narrows'. This had been preceded by a typically idiosyncratic (on Jones's part) and as yet unpublished correspondence that is described in Roland Mathias's introduction to the separate publication of the poem by Interim Press in 1981.

V

Poems continued to appear, not frequently but steadily, during the period of his editorship, a few in AWR, others in magazines such as POETRY WALES, MABON and AKROS. In 1971 they were gathered in ABSALOM IN THE TREE. It is interesting to speculate why he chose the title, since the title poem (one of a group of three that are essentially dramatic monologues) does not represent the pervading mood of the book. In 'Absalom' the familiar Bible story is largely taken as understood; what we have is its conclusion, in five tightly organized stanzas with a little, regular rhyme and a repeated refrain: *Cut me down*. This Absalom is a man full of words. Suspended in his tree, he has lost feeling in scalp and limbs, but not his rebel pride or his rhetoric. There is no pretence of regret or of sorrow, even for himself. His self-advocacy is the common demand of youth for the freedoms age enjoys; he does not relish the prospect of his father's forgiveness if he is cut down alive. The one who stops beneath the tree is Joab, his father's general, who has a sharp sword and blunt intentions.

'Indictment' and 'For Jenkin Jones Prisoner at Carmarthen, These' share with 'Absalom' an actorly panache. They are in the line of certain earlier poems that are as fitted for the stage as they are for the page. Although based on historical or biblical characters and events ('Indictment', a product of the research for WHITSUN RIOT, being almost a 'found' poem), they do not need explication of background particulars to impress the reader. In form they differ, but each is charged with verbal energy. Roland Mathias's Absalom could not wheedle: *Cut me down* is nearer an order than a plea. The interrogator of John Arnold (or Arnallt), in 'Indictment', to whom the poet has given questions Paul Delahay drafted in 1601, is obviously playing to the gallery, and though 'For Jenkin Jones' is somewhat quieter in tone, to represent the persona of Henry Vaughan in his study, the display of language is still vigorous.

The book contains a group of poems inspired by a visit to Brittany. Two focus on contrasts between past and present. In 'Au Cimetière de Brest' the noise of supermarket loudspeakers carries over the plots of the grand, memorialized dead. The death in 'A Celtic Death' is that of the Breton way of life, in its final throes on the Isle of Ouessant, where old people watch the weekly haemorrhage of the young to work and school in Brest. 'The Fool in the Wood' has more personal significance. It is technically complex and has been much worked over, because its purpose is confessional and penitential. Salaun, tree-dweller, holy fool, will utter only the Breton words *O Itroun Gerhez Mari*. When at last he falls from his perch and cracks his skull, his corpse pushes through the soil a lily that bears the same utterance in Latin, *Ave Maria*. The verbal reduction points a moral to a *glib* man

> smart to note
> Four Breton words glossed and struck
> To two Latinate, slower to look
> Piercingly at the cost and bloat
> I have of words. Four, two, less
> Than a fraction of one is their sure
> Count Godwards, alas, for lack of a pure
> Heart and a praising gentleness.

The self-examination is more rigorous and the verdict harder than any that would come from a critic.

Jeremy Hooker sees in the above poem and 'God Is' *urgent and remorseless expressions of . . . disquieting scrutiny.* 'God Is' reveals more: a reason for self-deprecation. This taut lyric of Blakeian intensity is an indictment of Christian inaction, worse in himself than others because he devotes his time to study. Much of the meaning of the poem turns upon the final word.

God is who questions me
Of my tranquillity
And works against the grain
To raise up Cain.

What is this mark I set
On each sleek head? The hot
Manifest of dislike or ice-
Pick of justice?

What are these books, this room
In which I sit so long?
Are we not met to cry
'Lord, justify!'

The commoner sense of 'justify' in theological discourse is to make righteous by the infusion of grace. But used in its earlier sense, as here, it means 'try as a judge'. Robbed of their poetry, the lines say, God asks me why I am so still and strives to raise me up. Do I simply show dislike of the plump and lubricious, or do I punish them? What is the purpose of such long study? Is not the only useful work to call for God's judgement. They are an uncompromising expression of Puritan belief.

With few exceptions, the other poems in ABSALOM are about mutability. The harsh messages of 'God Is' and 'The Fool in the Wood' are a consequence of confronting the inescapable: there is only so much time to do what needs to be done. An awareness of time comes with the loss of that unselfconscious haleness of body and energy, harbinger of the process of decline towards dissolution. Death figures in almost two-thirds of the poems in the book.

The keynote is sounded in 'Brynafan: First Light'. It is a half-waking nightmare that begins in black night with a presentiment of sudden death, digestion incomplete, and ends in grey but certain day, the fears of night over, with a wish that the inexorable passage of time be delayed *just long enough/For a last crack at ill.*

Brynafan (a cottage the poet's brother once owned in Cardiganshire) provides the rural setting, but there is a fox, which is also death, outside on the hill, *tod on his heap/Of ages*, and the blackness of a bedroom with its arched roof timbers brings a sequence of consonants like cracking bones to the first two lines – *Within the cruck the night/Is thick.* Other textual devices, occasional full and half-rhyme, internal rhyme and altered colloquial phrases, pin the poem together.

The sense of things not done, a true mark not made, and time running out, permeates 'A Letter from Gwyther Street'. The address is in Pembroke Dock and Raymond Garlick (in PLANET 9) identifies *Herbie and Doc/And Elis* as members of that circle of literary friends he and Roland shared in the town, in sunnier times, symbolized by the buried beach the poet's feet uncover in the opening lines of the poem. All now show the ravages of age and ill health. The old companionship can do nothing for them. The flow of the tide erasing the footprints in the sand reinforces the message: *as I looked back,/Not a mark of my passing anywhere*. In 'Sarnesfield', the graveside rites in the cemetery of the border village are interrupted by the hammering of a woodpecker. A companion's observation, *'You know/He only drills a dead branch, don't you?'* remains to haunt, even in sunlight, those who cannot know when they are marked for death.

The violent death of friends in a terrorist attack is commemorated in a beautifully crafted elegy 'Some Tight-lipped Wave', and there are elegiac poems for his father and his father's family, *That swarthy cenedl*. In 'They Have Not Survived' he traces the clan from *the melancholy/Rhos* to the mining valleys –

> *Coughing in terraces above*
> *The coal, their doorsteps whitened*
> *And the suds of pride draining*
> *Away down the numbered*
> *Steps to the dole . . .*

Like 'The Fool in the Wood', the poem ends in self-analysis and self-criticism. His *bloat . . . of words* has some purpose; he can speak for the exploited, stained as he is with the guilt of the exploiters.

> *For this dark cousinhood only I*
> *Can speak. Why am I unlike*

> *Them, alive and jack in office,*
> *Shrewd among the plunderers?*

'For an Unmarked Grave' is an elegy for the poet's uncle, his father's brother, who lived near Sennybridge. The last dozen lines, culminating in the contrast between the loss of the bereaved and nature's indifference to human mortality, are a triumph of that dramatic utterance that is the unmistakable voice of Roland Mathias.

> *How long is it,*
> *David, long since your loins were water,*
> *Since you were carpenter, wed, kept shop,*
> *Were poor and a theologian, companied*
> *A nephew wide over Senni and the nearer*
> *Hill of day? Nothing to tell,*
> *No fossil couplet . . .?*

The autumnal gloom and pitiless self-questioning that characterize many of these poems is absent from 'A Last Respect', which describes his father's funeral cortège winding slowly to the chapel graveyard at Aber. It is a summer's day, the weather *just/For a last progress*, sunny and still. The dusty hedgerows and the mountains rising above, *the pinnacles/Of Sion*, catch the poet's eye, not the flooded valley below. The sudden arrival of a gust of wind seems to be a sign:

> *all*
> *But the elm and the brass handles had air*
> *About it and petals flying, impassioned as*
> *Wings . . .*

There is a final question, but it is one that invites the reader to share in an affirmation of faith –

Who are you to say that my father, wily
And old in the faith, had not in that windflash abandoned
His fallen minister's face?

Absalom was ignored by London reviewers and
given scant notice elsewhere. The Western Mail
drew on Jeremy Hooker's critical survey of the
earlier books (in the summer 1971 number of Poetry
Wales), which had found the obscurity of some
poems *maddening*, and dismissed it without troub-
ling to turn the pages. In Planet, damning with faint
praise, the reviewer found *signs of effort . . . addiction
to the resonance of his own language . . . qualified by a
spare kind of self-regard.* In AWR, Peter Abbs balanced
praise for the *convincing and urgent rhythms of speech*
with criticism of poems in which he discovered *an
unpalatable mixture of cliché, abstraction and rhetoric.*

The Western Mail reviewer could not have known
that, having read Absalom, Jeremy Hooker would
change his mind, would see in it indeed *an access of
clarity*, and begin a re-evaluation of the poet. Now he
saw him in that tradition of English verse in which
the individual sounds and arrangements of words
(that texturing that Roland assiduously practised)
contribute to meaning. He recognized also that critical to many of the poems was a conflict between the
poet as artificer with words and the man with a
powerful moral conscience. Hooker's review, in
Poetry Wales, winter 1971, ends almost on a note of
apology: what in the early books had been considered irritatingly difficult was now seen to have
been insufficiently considered.

When in 1972 Absalom was awarded the Welsh Arts
Council's prize for poetry, it was partial restitution

as well as formal recognition of work that was original, technically inventive, profound and moving.

The small compass of this essay does not permit more than cursory acknowledgement of the many facets of Roland's life after his retirement as headmaster – among them, his lay-preaching, his chairmanship of the English-language Section of Yr Academi Gymreig and of the Literature Committee of the Welsh Arts Council, his occasional broadcasts, his work as visiting lecturer in colleges of the University of Wales and at universities in Brittany and the United States, culminating in the honorary doctorate he received from the University of Georgetown, DC, in 1985. Nor is it possible to do adequate justice to his literary criticism and scholarly writing for books and journals.

This latter part of his output includes major contributions, to ANATOMY OF WALES (1972) and THE WELSH LANGUAGE TODAY (1973). The former, entitled 'Thin Spring and Tributary', has a fine sweep of argument, supported by historical fact, that establishes comprehensively the origins of Anglo-Welsh writing in the twentieth century. The latter, 'The Welsh Language and the English Language', is very largely about the shifting pattern of linguistic boundaries in Wales from about 500 BC to the present. With a wealth of historical and literary reference it describes how, down the centuries, in various parts of Wales and in neighbouring counties over the border, tides of Welsh or English have washed over watersheds and up and down valleys, swelled close to the skirts of feudal towns and ebbed away again. It tells also of the influences of religion, industrialization and education on language choice and preservation, and the hastening decline of Welsh in the twentieth century. Both essays are ultimately concerned with *a profound need to assess the requirements of* [the English-speaking] *majority in a bilingual Wales*, which the writer considers culturally deprived. He sees a *rift between the culture of Welsh-speaking Wales, which has its complementary areas, folk and intellectual, and the deprived English-only majority, which has no folk culture at all except an echo of mid-Atlantic postures and a significant, if small, intellectual culture which schools and universities have largely ignored.*

He was pleased to note in 1973 developments such as the availability of a few optional courses in Anglo-Welsh literature in higher education institutions, but he was driven to conclude that *the deadly circle of ignorance and indifference has been dented not broken.* This gloomy assessment was not made an excuse for inactivity – rather the opposite. With increased vigour he pursued his vocation to raise the status of Welsh writing in English and inform and educate the potential public for it in Wales. Serious critics, he argued, needed to recognize the special qualities of the Welsh-English background and its historical and literary ancestry. The other major essays, conveniently collected in A RIDE THROUGH THE WOOD (1985) are, like his painstaking reviews, elements in a prolonged demonstration of taking Anglo-Welsh literature seriously, as a manifestation of a distinctive society in need of understanding.

Roland Mathias's image of Anglo-Welsh writing as a wood in which he will guide the earnest traveller to unexpected delights beyond the more commonly known periphery may seem romantic and has been misunderstood by some critics. These suspect it

91

betrays an unwillingness to come to terms with the modern world. It is true that none of the essays is about the younger generation in Anglo-Welsh literature, or urban industrial Wales, but that was not the writer's intention. He wanted to take readers directly to some of the key figures and issues in studies composed *with difficulty and such care as I could muster.*

With one exception, a survey of Anglo-Welsh poets in the nineteenth century, the essays were written to commission. Five were originally lectures or addresses, four were requested by other editors as contributions to a collection of critical studies or special numbers of magazines. In the main, they belong to the period 1971–81. They by no means represent the whole of his output of this kind during the decade. He rarely declined a commission or an invitation to speak, and as he was incapable of less than meticulous preparation and undertook what other writers might dismiss as hack work with care and love, the invitations came frequently. These essays are, however, his selection of the most important.

He emerges as the most productive among Anglo-Welsh critics and arguably the most perceptive. His severe intellectual scrutiny confronts every difficulty and he consistently challenges the writer's intention from a strong moral base. He explores David Jones's extraordinary layered learning and his fluid handling of time and produces a coherent view of his art. This he sees as founded in the writer's childhood affiliation to Wales and a concept of continuity from the culture of antiquity which stands above the imperatives of contemporary politics. 'Lord

Cutglass, Twenty Years After' is a lively and convincing analysis of Dylan Thomas's essential Englishness and recessive exploitation of childhood in maturity. Here too is an assessment of UNDER MILK WOOD that gives the play its due but refuses to acknowledge depth and complexity where neither exist. He is both a strong admirer of the work of R. S. Thomas and one of his most searching judges. His scrupulous reading offers insights into the essential solitariness of Thomas and the challenges of doubt and contradiction that constantly beset him. He finds a failure of philosophical coherence in the view the poems present of God and the workings of nature, and confusion of beauty and grace, and over the influence that nature and art should have on the wholeness and morality of man. Understandably, he cannot close his eyes to R. S. Thomas's devaluation of the contribution that the Nonconformist chapels have made to Welsh life. Emyr Humphreys he finds a more companionable figure. The article 'Channels of Grace', reprinted in A RIDE THROUGH THE WOOD, has been referred to above in its first printed version in AWR No. 70. It is worth remarking further of the essay in this context that it draws an interesting comparison between Humphreys's essential seriousness and that which emerges in the work of Alun Lewis. Roland develops the argument to support his thesis that *there was something in the community of Wales . . . in the past three centuries that made such seriousness about the salvation of the world or of the individual or both a preoccupation – an idea that one would never glean from twentieth century caricatures of the Puritan community . . .*

The first of two important essays on Lewis, 'The Black Spot in the Focus', rebuts the common critical view of him as a poet blown about by the winds of fate and blasted by the war before he could attain a steady vision. Roland shows him whole and consistent, as an idealist, an international socialist, bred in a family conditioned by Dissent if no longer part of it, in whose agnostic outlook Christian thought and imagery persist. He traces the phases of the development of Lewis's faith in the survival of Love to the dreadful realization that its healing would be postponed beyond his lifetime. 'The Caseg Letters: A Commentary' is chiefly about the centrality of Wales to Alun Lewis's thinking – again a new direction in critical thought. In a long introductory section he analyses with patient scholarship the National Library's collection of the poet's correspondence with Brenda Chamberlain, who had edited it for her book, THE MAKING OF THE CASEG BROADSHEETS. The essay shows that as well as correcting the letters, she occasionally altered and omitted passages, and changed the chronological sequence. Roland rescues the full meaning from the adulterated version to chart the progress in the poet's thinking, and to reveal the truth of his peroration in his final letter from India. This reassessment of the Caseg enterprise reveals Alun Lewis's declaration of his allegiance to Wales, and his belief in the necessity of radical politics and education, and in the role of artists to elevate humanity by bringing their art into society.

Vernon Watkins is another essential feature of 'The Main Ride'. As his review of THE DEATH BELL (1954) in DOCK LEAVES made plain, Roland did not greatly care for the way Watkins's poetry was developing at that time. He held the earlier books, up to THE LADY WITH THE UNICORN, in high regard, and when, in

1971, he was invited to contribute to Triskel One, a collection of essays on Welsh and Anglo-Welsh literature, he saw an opportunity to explain his view and to elucidate poems that Watkins himself had steadfastly refused to shed light upon. In a characteristically patient and erudite study, 'Grief and the Circus Horse', he explores the Christian and mythic themes in the poetry of his erstwhile companion at University College, Swansea, who had died in Seattle four years previously.

Roland Mathias probably knows more of the intricate craft of Vernon Watkins, by study and intuition, than any other critic. Though very different in temperament and in their attitude to history, they have a good deal in common – a public-school education of about the same period (Watkins's Repton was Anglican whereas Caterham was Congregationalist) and Oxbridge, the gift of a retentive memory, a grounding in the classics, a mind well stocked by extensive reading in literature and philosophy – and a delight in walking and the natural world, and outdoor sports. The Triskel One essay enabled a significant advance in the ordinary reader's understanding of Watkins. It explained the poet's philosophy, compounded of Christianity and Platonism, and his arcane symbol system (the fountain, the river, the gnat dance, the foal) and made accessible that extraordinary dramatic poem 'Ballad of the Mari Lwyd'.

Three years later Roland turned again to Watkins, in his 'Writers of Wales' monograph on the poet. On this occasion he had room to outline Watkins's family background and the origin of his poetic preoccupation with the conquest of time in his grief for the death of youth. He describes his life, preternaturally dedicated to poetry almost from infancy, and examines the major influences on Watkins's writing, especially Yeats, the friendship with Dylan Thomas, the place of nature in the poetry, the obsessive refinement of poems, and the later achievement of a more orthodox Christian position. The book provides a comprehensive treatment of a metaphysical poet who habitually disguised emotion and often added a further dimension of difficulty to what was already obscure by reworking poems many years after they were first composed and thus dissociated from their initial impetus. Given the subject, it is a triumph of lucidity.

VI

In his preface to A RIDE THROUGH THE WOOD Roland
Mathias explains that he excluded an essay on John
Cowper Powys because he wished to concentrate on
the work of *unmistakably Anglo-Welsh writers*. The
text he thus dismissed may well have been that of a
lecture he gave to the Powys Society in the summer
of 1973. This led to an invitation to write a fuller
study, which, fitted into the interstices of a crowded
life, took a considerable time. However, when THE
HOLLOWED-OUT ELDER STALK appeared from Enitharmon Press in 1979, it was a comprehensive treatment of John Cowper Powys as a poet.

The book combines biography, analysis of the
unusual psychology of the writer and contextual-
ization and explication of the poetry, most of which
was written and published in the United States and,
until quite recently, available only there. The chronological organization of the work allows the reader to
pursue the philosophical and poetic development of
this highly idiosyncratic late-Romantic. It may
appear rather odd that Roland should take for his
subject this half-pagan writer with a taste for the
dramatically bizarre and a highly personal perspective of history. However, Cowper Powys the novelist
of Wessex and, later, of a fantastic historical Wales,
had long held a fascination for him. There was interest, too, in a poet who had an *unfailing attachment to
tight rhyme schemes and stanza structures*, and who
shared his love of the landscape of home, the wind,
the weather and foliage wet with rain, recollected

though they were in hotel rooms in arid American states.

The book involved extensive researching and reading about Cowper Powys's family and the classical mythology and philosophy that inform his work. The influences on his poetry are traced – Wordsworth, early Yeats, Milton, Keats, Tennyson and Arnold, and oddly, at Hardy's prompting, Edgar Allan Poe, whose rhythm and sound effects as well as the preoccupation with the death wish had a strong appeal.

The outcome is literary criticism of a high order. The wide range of reference is mastered and organized with every appearance of ease, judgements of quality are clear, and issues, whether of philosophy or technique, are tackled firmly. The writing is lucid and the subject emerges many-sided and whole.

Roland Mathias has always been generous in his support of other writers and editors. Between 1978 when the project began and 1986 when it was brought to a successful conclusion, he gave a great deal of his time and erudition to THE OXFORD COMPANION TO THE LITERATURE OF WALES. Meic Stephens, editor of the COMPANION, pays warm tribute to him as one of the five major contributors of entries and as meticulous reader of the whole text. During this period he also collaborated with Raymond Garlick to compile what has become a standard anthology, ANGLO-WELSH POETRY 1480–1980, and was engaged in writing ANGLO-WELSH LITERATURE: AN ILLUSTRATED HISTORY. Both these books have an educational purpose. With the former, published in 1984, the editors realized their long-held ambition to see an anthology of the kind available cheaply to schools and colleges, where experience had taught them that Anglo-Welsh literature was usually badly resourced and neglected.

In his reviews of illustrated books Roland Mathias set high standards: illustrations had to be pertinent and suitably placed with reference to the text. The HISTORY (published in 1986) meets these requirements and as a scholarly survey it has other claims to being distinctively personal. Almost half the book is devoted to the twentieth century. The remainder charts the uncertain progress of the Anglo-Welsh towards the modern world. The view of Wales propagated about the time of the Treachery of the Blue Books, he argues, had a debilitating effect on truly Anglo-Welsh writers. In prose they cultivated antiquarianism or the *lunatic darkness* of pseudo-history, and their poetry has *an apologetic sound.* At the beginning of the twentieth century, it is perhaps understandable that dislike of Lloyd George should have given rise to anti-Welsh books by English authors. That Caradoc Evans should have exploited such writing for revenge and commercial gain is less acceptable, especially as his example of a highly selective and eccentric portrayal of Wales and Welsh characters was followed by Anglo-Welsh writers for thirty years or more.

The critical observations offered on pre-twentieth-century writing are, within the scope of the book, necessarily brief in the main; those on major twentieth-century figures are substantial and, on occasion, unexpectedly critical. As ever, his judgement is acute and owes nothing to the influence of others:

To re-read the early numbers of WALES, *which created a verbal furore between 1937 and 1940, is to realise that those who still talk of a 'golden era' then are misled by a temporary English market judgement, which a longer perspective cannot possibly support. The London appetite for Welsh eccentricities – not to mention the eccentricities themselves – has died long since.*

This, however, is not to depreciate the new wave of the 'First Flowering', which he describes as *deep and rich*. In its aftermath, the war over, there was for a long time very little of report. The first twelve years of THE ANGLO-WELSH REVIEW were *dispiriting*. Raymond Garlick left for Holland. It was in large part a matter of readership:

The English-reading public of Wales, largely dependent on London newspapers, followed the wider readership of England in believing that there never had been Anglo-Welsh writing of importance except from the pen of Dylan Thomas, and he was dead.

The dark hours of the 1950s and the signs and substance of new dawn are the themes of Roland's chapter on 'Literature in English' in THE ARTS IN WALES 1950–1975 (edited by Meic Stephens). The HISTORY necessarily recapitulates the characters and events of this era and brings the conspectus up to date. With the beginning of the funding of literature by the Arts Council in 1963, the emergence of new leaders like Meic Stephens, and the re-emergence of some older writers, a new energy found expression in what he terms *The Second Movement*. At the end of the book Roland sees the prospect of many more writers coming forward with each generation in south-east Wales and wherever Welsh has receded, and promising signs in contemporary Anglo-Welsh literature of writing in English being brought into direct and fruitful contact with the Welsh literary and historic tradition.

The critical judgement and the hopeful vision are both characteristic, as are those long-standing interests of the author that the reader of AN ILLUSTRATED HISTORY will readily identify. The book begins with a display of erudition about the shifting language frontiers of Wales; Madoc and the Welsh Indians find a place, as does Robert Scourfield Mills, who, in the guise of Captain Owen Vaughan (or Owen Rhoscomyl) wrote THE LONE TREE LODE and brought a sense of Welshness to Roland Mathias as a boy. In the second half of the book, David Jones, Vernon Watkins and Emyr Humphreys are among several writers given particular attention, and Alun Lewis is again identified as the tragically lost leader of Anglo-Welsh literature.

The name of Merthyr is most frequently repeated in the survey of twentieth-century writing, but Brecon and the border loom large in the treatment of Anglo-Welsh antecedents, pre-eminent among whom is Henry Vaughan. In the HISTORY, Vaughan is described as *one of the great metaphysicals*. The claim is undisputed, but it was not arrived at lightly; Vaughan had long been one of Roland Mathias's special interests. In preparing A RIDE THROUGH THE WOOD, he had been stimulated by an essay he contributed to the Henry Vaughan special number of POETRY WALES in 1975 to recommence research on the subject. The first fruits appear in the the paragraphs on Vaughan in the HISTORY.

'The Silurist Pursued', an unfinished work, was

conceived as a book-length study designed to answer the question, why 'Silurist'? The beginnings of the answer bring together details of the Vaughans' rather unsavoury family background and a brief history of the Silures, late arrivals in Britain who added names like Llanfihangel vibon Avel to the landscape from their own Celtic tongue but, more significantly, were in later centuries the most loyal subjects and soldiers of English kings. The study focuses on Henry Vaughan as a staunch Royalist, close associate of Sir Herbert Price of the Priory in Brecon and the Digbys of Coleshill in the Midlands. The poet is pursued through the circles in which he moved, the friends for whom he wrote, the hermetic philosophy he read, and the movements of his times, not specifically literary, in which he became involved. It is shown that, although he spoke Welsh, Vaughan had little sympathy for the anti-Royalist mass of the people and little knowledge of the cultural heritage of Wales. The claim that Vaughan's poetry was influenced by bardic measures and techniques is shown to be without foundation. At this point, where studies of the poet were being taken in a new direction, the typescript breaks off.

Roland Mathias's last book of poems, SNIPE'S CASTLE, was published in 1979. It might well have included 'New Lease', which comes at the end of ABSALOM IN THE TREE, but like many poems in SNIPE'S CASTLE draws its inspiration from Pembrokeshire. At one level, 'New Lease' is about the poet's acquisition of a run-down cottage in St Twynell's; the first words are, almost verbatim, those of a sanitary inspector surveying the property. The reference to Llifiau, the Pict who, in *The Gododdin*, joined the warriors of Mynyddog Mwynfawr to fight against the Angles at

Catraeth, is a sign of deeper meaning. The poet's image of himself, *crass/As a pict and no less/Mercenary*, is typically ungenerous to his own motives, but not to keep and care for the house will clearly be dereliction of a fundamental responsibility. The house is more than a house. 'New Lease' recalls the lines of Waldo Williams, a Pembrokeshire poet, *Beth yw gwladgarwch? Cadw tŷ/Mewn cwmwl tystion* (What is love of country? Keeping house/In a cloud of witnesses).

Love of country (as distinct from love of landscape) often expressed in scholarly obsession with its distinctive origins, history and culture, permeates a great deal of Roland Mathias's prose, but it appears late in the poetry, and most obviously in four poems in SNIPE'S CASTLE, including the title poem. The emotional and intellectual ties to Wales are strong, but not unquestioned. The theme is clearly presented in 'Porth Cwyfan', where the surface detail is simple enough: a cold June morning; a dog barking, nonsensically angry, guarding a place with which it has no connection of ownership; a walk along a spit of sand to the island and Cwyfan's neglected chapel; a gravestone to one Roger Parry; a couple with their child on the beach, Lancastrians, who ask *Can/We get to the island?*; and in response an anger as irrational as the dog's. This reaction is the *small/Inevitable tragedy, the umpteenth/In a sinuous month*, that the poem analyses. Does knowledge of history grant territorial right that can be angrily withheld from those who do not possess it?

> *. . . how is my tripright sounder,*
> *Save that I know Roger Parry and he does not?*

Resentment of tourists and incomers to Wales cannot be accepted unquestioningly. In the title poem, invasion is examined from a fresh perspective. The Snipe's Castle of the poem is a ruined cottage not far from the poet's own in Pembrokeshire. The poem supplies an explanation for the name when neighbours cannot. It considers the defensive connotation and the possible source of threat

> *. . . in that backward era*
> *Preseli would come up pat to a Little*
> *England eye . . .*

As 'castle' starts a train of images, so does 'snipe'. There is a certain playfulness in the play on words, but the humour is barbed. The *egregious* Snipe is imagined *grudging the time of day/To countrymen longer billed and taxed than you/A lot:* a wealthy and distant 'little Englander'.

There is a similar contrast, but more harshly drawn, in 'Is it the Same Country?', where the profitable strawberry fields are placed side by side with the land that bred his father's family, the barren squatter's moor of 'They Have Not Survived' in ABSALOM. There is anger in the poem, in the final lines of biblically apocalyptic dimensions, but it is generated as much by self-reproof as by a sense of injustice. The poet sees himself *deer stalkered* (and later, *in my vented coat/And ear-flaps*), still *shrewd/ Among the plunderers –*

> *by the coining road*
> *From England and nowhere . . .*

In this poem, too, *house* has symbolic force. It stands for the Wales (idiomatically identified by *the fallen*

104

pine-end . . . of an old house) that he seeks, not peopled by *strangers/Alert for other strangers*, with an eye to *pillage*, but a hard land where *the lofty precept* must do for wealth.

In an article entitled 'Pe medrwn yr iaith . . .' in Y FANER (February 1980), Roland Mathias began by saying that he regretted that, for all his attendance at Welsh classes, he still could not speak the language –

a minnau ag awydd mor gryf i fedru siarad Cymraeg, a throi mewn cylchoedd le'i siaredir, a chael yr ymdeimlad o fod 'i fewn' yn y Gymru etifeddol.
(and I with so strong a desire to be able to speak Welsh, and to move in circles where it is spoken, and to have the feeling of sharing fully in the heritage of Wales.)

The same regret finds expression in 'To a Tombstone Fragment in the Garden Path'. The remnant of the Welsh inscription on the stone conveys little except national identity (*you still have a nation*); it is a link with his own heritage that the poet is unable to make. Broken as it is, the stone is preserved, face up, a memorative talisman conjured in the final lines to forge the connection anew:

> *I who would quickly refashion*
> *My stony fathers, had I learned*
> *But how, call you to speak,*
> *Speak.*

The vast tract of Welsh and Celtic cultural heritage he commanded supplied the scholarly detail of 'La Tène' and the long dramatic poem 'Madoc'. The former is in part an animadversion on the tourist industry, but its theme is ultimately craftsmanship – that of the intricate metal worker of the Celtic past and his own in the present as poet.

> These later deals
> Of mine are in words: my quick and unshelved wish
> Is to sell each one from a mould made new
> In the speaking.

The self-analysis is typically unflinching: he, like the Celt, has debased skill to make *just what/The buyers need*.

If the later poems of ABSALOM and SNIPE'S CASTLE are more accessible, their meanings less concealed *with/ Leaves curling lost faces and the throes of old/Tragedy curved into birds and cubs*, there is still no compromise with intellectual honesty and challenge. 'Madoc', as broadcast, is a stern test for the listener.

The Welsh Arts Council–BBC commission to write a long poem for radio gave Roland the opportunity to display his knowledge about the Madoc controversy. While the historian might conclude the legend 'unproven' or 'unlikely', the poet's imagination can place Madoc's followers in America, in conflict with the native inhabitants. Gwenllian represents those who would battle to preserve pure the heritage of Wales; the men fight only while there is hope of victory and, with defeat inevitable, mingle blood, language and traditions with those of the Indians. John Evans of Waunfawr, sent to investigate the rumours of Welsh Indians, finds himself beset on all sides by colonizers with political and commercial claims. He will serve neither England's king nor Spain and denies a hint of Welshness in the Mandans. But Chief Big White of the Mandans and George Catlin, the artist who painted Mandan village life, provide the evidence that Evans will not. The setting is an Indian heaven where time has no meaning: characters from different centuries speak. Though they address and hear one another, progression is not by conventional dialogue, but rather in dramatic monologues of the kind long part of the poet's repertoire (and represented elsewhere in this book by 'Sir Gelli to R.S.'). There is opposition of ideas, between Gwenllian's fierce defence of language and distinctive culture at all costs and the way of peace and survival at the expense of dilution of identity. The story of the Welsh Indians is an allegory of the predicament of Wales which, as other poems in SNIPE'S CASTLE show, had become a concern of increasing importance. Peace has been from his youth an article of faith for Roland Mathias, but in the conflict of cultures the choice is not simple.

> *Perhaps our choice is always*
> *Between a vacuous and piebald peace*
> *And a clash of fiery disciplines.*

Intellectual honesty and religious conviction are in the end the twin pillars of his being in art and life. The starting-point of writing in these later poems is, as it always was, the natural world, but the syntax and diction are generally more accessible, and the images and symbols more readily comprehended. The rhythms and idioms of colloquial speech, skilfully woven into the texture of lines, occur more frequently.

These characteristics are present in 'A Stare from the Mountain', where, although the first sentence extends over fifteen lines, it presents no obscurity

and a colloquial phrase is enfolded in sustained patterning of vowels and consonants:

> As the sun slants, the best of it over,
> Into the trug of Usk from the summary
> West, masking the struts, the wicker rents
> With plush, with a stuff of shaded
> Greens . . .

It is the setting of an epiphany, in the unlikely form
of a *portly grassblown . . . pony* that, standing between
him and the declining sun, is haloed – *Marked with
redemption*. The town below, steeped in history, is lit
by the sun and saved (even the rubbish tip is refined
by a plume of smoke), but, searching himself, he sees
no sign that he is redeemed.

An exact description of 'Burning Brambles' is unexpectedly brought off in rhyming couplets, the
flexible long lines imitating the *rooting whips* of the
brambles themselves. There is a glint of light in this
poem too, from the distant sea, but the *new heart*
from which it seems to anticipate response is not
there, for *the land is unhealthy*. The images of waste
have a deeper meaning. Old bottles are *a heap of old
sins without consequence, save/Deep in the land's heart*.
The poet's self-excoriation parallels the *slow excoria-
tion* of the brambles, *mindless as snakes but bitter*, and
concludes with the harshest of judgements:

> It is enough to unpile and shift
> The endless loops of this waste, hearing the crackle behind
> And knowing the smell of a life ill lived as it passes down wind.

'Brechfa Chapel' has a different perspective. It looks
at Christianity under threat and finds neither solace

nor hope. The poem begins with a description of a natural scene, peopled with birds, coot, swan and gulls, whose behaviours are personified, especially the gulls, *shifting/Like pillagers . . . testy . . . a militant brabble*, with their *Hatred of strangers*. Inscriptions on stones in the graveyard and the chapel itself raise questions about the dwindling of faith and its continued survival: *Is the old witness done?* The anxious coot and the dreaming swan, touched by light but oblivious of threat, are emblems of Christian attitudes, while the *hellish noise* of the gulls is *harrying the conversation/Of faith*. The chapel is cared for, but the farmers in their self-contained practice of religion are keeping alive a habit of ritual from which the meaning of Christian fellowship is receding. The poem offers its desolate answer to the fragmentation of the faithful:

> *Each on his own must stand and conjure*
> *The strong remembered words, the unanswerable*
> *Texts against chaos.*

A number of Roland Mathias's poems were set to music by Mansel Thomas, a friend of many years, and David Harries. It was David Harries who invited his collaboration on a cantata for the Fishguard Festival in July 1979. This was the genesis of 'Tide Reach', the sequence of poems that concludes SNIPE'S CASTLE. Locations in the poems are on the peninsula south of Milford Haven where he had his cottage, many within easy walking distance of it, but they are seen at points in time between the fifth century ('Guénolé') and the present ('The Arming of Aberdaugleddau'). The perspective of history is inherent in him and he is steeped in the history of Pembrokeshire – he had used it in celebration twenty years earlier in his

Festival of Wales pageant. This is a very different work. It is responsive to music in its variety of technical devices: patterns of rhyme and repetition, long and short lines, questions and answers, choruses, differing moods and voices.

The sequence shares with many of the later poems precise observation of the natural world that is also emblematic. There is perhaps an apprehension of the immanence of God in land and seascapes that are usually bleak rather than beautiful or, if not that, they are object lessons and instruments in the rigour of self-examination. The two poems that frame the sequence are different however, most obviously in that they offer praise and hope. They carry the burden of the poet's endeavour to give a religious connotation to the whole. 'The Green Chapel' is a parable, one furthermore that commands us to look, to see, in the destruction of the cliff by the waves and simultaneous creation of a buttress of rock poised against the cliff, a lesson of paradoxes – of strength in weakness, needing in being needed. In this poem the presence of God is indeed in *the shapen stillness of rock* and the *Effort the water makes*, and the endlessness of the process is an emblem of immortality.

The concluding poem, 'Laus Deo', is an achievement of extraordinary power and beauty. It draws together the threads of history and celebration of this favourite part of Wales in a fusing of love of God and love of the country God preserves. The land and sea are seen as they are, both bleak and bountiful; history brings its quota of *Hard hands* and *high/Heads* to lay hold on *this old domain*, but they cannot keep it. At the heart of the poem are the lovely lines

> *It is one engrossing work, this frail*
> *Commerce of souls in a corner,*
> *Its coming and going, and the mark*
> *Of the temporal on it*

before the peroration

> *It is one*
> *Coherent work, this Wales*
> *And the seaway of Wales, its Maker*
> *As careful of strength as*
> *Of weakness, its quirk and cognomen*
> *And trumpet allowed for*
> *The whole peninsula's length.*
> *It is one affirmative work, this Wales*
> *And the seaway of Wales.*

SNIPE'S CASTLE received lengthy and considered reviews and brought Roland Mathias the wider recognition as a poet he had long merited. When it came out in 1983, BURNING BRAMBLES, a selection of the poems he had published between 1944 and 1979, was equally well-received. In an article he wrote for POETRY WALES (Vol. 21, 1985), Jeremy Hooker re-examined the poetry as a whole and placed Roland firmly in the Puritan tradition. BRITISH BOOK NEWS declared *Mathias is an underestimated artist.*

As well as the Henry Vaughan research, he had poems on the stocks in 1985 when he was taken ill. Since then he has been flexing his intellectual muscles by sorting and categorizing many years of carefully hoarded papers and correspondence. This essay is greatly indebted to that labour.

In 1992 the poems began to appear again.

A Selected Bibliography

Poetry

Days Enduring and Other Poems, Ilfracombe: Stockwell, 1943.

Break in Harvest and Other Poems, London: Routledge, 1946.

The Roses of Tretower, Pembroke Dock: Dock Leaves Press, 1952.

The Flooded Valley, London: Putnam, 1960.

Absalom in the Tree and Other Poems, Llandysul: Gomer, 1971.

Snipe's Castle, Llandysul: Gomer, 1979.

Burning Brambles: Selected Poems 1944–1979, Llandysul: Gomer, 1983.

Prose

The Eleven Men of Eppynt and Other Stories, Pembroke Dock: Dock Leaves Press, 1956.

Whitsun Riot: An Account of a Commotion Amongst Catholics in Herefordshire and Monmouthshire in 1605, London: Bowes and Bowes 1963.

VERNON WATKINS (Writers of Wales series), Cardiff: University of Wales Press, 1973.

THE HOLLOWED-OUT ELDER STALK: JOHN COWPER POWYS AS POET, London: Enitharmon, 1979.

A RIDE THROUGH THE WOOD: ESSAYS ON ANGLO-WELSH LITERATURE, Bridgend: Poetry Wales Press, 1985.

ANGLO-WELSH LITERATURE: AN ILLUSTRATED HISTORY, Bridgend: Poetry Wales Press, 1987.

Major Prose Contributions to Books Edited by Others

'In a Co-educational Grammar School in Wales', in THE SCHOOL AS A CHRISTIAN COMMUNITY, edited by W. O. Lester Smith, London: SCM Press, 1954.

'Thin Spring and Tributary', in ANATOMY OF WALES, edited by R. Brinley Jones, Peterston super Ely: Gwerin Publications, 1972.

'The Welsh Language and the English Language', in THE WELSH LANGUAGE TODAY, edited by Meic Stephens, Llandysul: Gomer, 1973.

Unattributed entries in THE OXFORD COMPANION TO THE LITERATURE OF WALES, edited by Meic Stephens, Oxford: Oxford University Press, 1986.

'The First Civil War' and 'The Second Civil War and Interregnum', chapters VI and VII in PEMBROKESHIRE COUNTY HISTORY, VOL. III edited by Brian Howells, Haverfordwest: Pembrokeshire Historical Society, 1987.

Biographical

Chapter by Roland Mathias in ARTISTS IN WALES, edited by Meic Stephens, Llandysul: Gomer, 1971.

Editorial Work

THE ANGLO-WELSH REVIEW from Vol. 11 No. 27, 1962, to Vol. 25 No. 56, 1976.

THE SHINING PYRAMID AND OTHER STORIES BY WELSH AUTHORS, edited by Sam Adams and Roland Mathias, Llandysul: Gomer, 1970.

THE COLLECTED SHORT STORIES OF GERAINT GOODWIN, edited by Sam Adams and Roland Mathias, Tenby: Five Arches Press, 1976.

ANGLO-WELSH POETRY, 1480–1980, edited by Raymond Garlick and Roland Mathias, Bridgend: Poetry Wales Press, 1984.

Reviews and Critical Studies of the Work of Roland Mathias

Article by Jeremy Hooker on 'The Poetry of Roland Mathias', in POETRY WALES, Vol. 7 No. 1, 1971.

Article by Jeremy Hooker on 'Roland Mathias: The Strong Remembered Words', in POETRY WALES, Vol. 21 No. 1, 1985.

Reviews

THE FLOODED VALLEY, by Glyn Jones, in THE ANGLO-WELSH REVIEW, No. 26, 1960.

ABSALOM IN THE TREE, by Peter Abbs, in AWR, No. 47, 1972; by Thomas Crawford in LINES REVIEW, No. 41, 1972; by Robin Fulton in PLANET, No. 10, 1972; by Jeremy Hooker in POETRY WALES, Vol. 7 No. 3, 1971.

SNIPE'S CASTLE, by Peter Elfed Lewis, in POETRY WALES, Vol. 15 No. 3, 1979/80; by Leslie Norris in THE POWYS REVIEW, No. 6, 1979/80.

BURNING BRAMBLES, by Anne Stevenson, in AWR, No. 76, 1984.

A RIDE THROUGH THE WOOD, by Jeremy Hooker, in POETRY WALES, Vol. 21 No. 4, 1986.

A complete bibliography of the works of Roland Mathias is included in John Harris, A BIBLIO-GRAPHICAL GUIDE TO TWENTY-FOUR MODERN ANGLO-WELSH WRITERS, Cardiff: University of Wales Press, 1994.

Acknowledgements

I am glad to acknowledge my deep indebtedness to Roland and Molly Mathias for many kindnesses over the years and especially for the extraordinary thoughtfulness and generosity of their assistance to me in the preparation of this essay.

The Author

Sam Adams is a native of Gilfach Goch in Glamorgan. He obtained an honours degree and an MA in English from University College of Wales, Aberystwyth.

Formerly a Senior Lecturer at Caerleon College of Education, he is now an Inspector of Schools for Her Majesty's Inspectorate.

He is a former editor of the magazine POETRY WALES, and a former chairman of the English-language section of Yr Academi Gymreig.

With Roland Mathias, he co-edited THE SHINING PYRAMID AND OTHER STORIES BY WELSH AUTHORS (Gomer, 1970), and was editor of TEN ANGLO-WELSH POETS (Carcanet, 1974). He wrote the volume on GERAINT GOODWIN for the Writers of Wales Series (UWP, 1975), and has published a volume of poetry entitled JOURNEYING (Gomer, 1974).

Designed by Jeff Clements
Typesetting at the University of Wales Press in
11pt Palatino and printed in Great Britain by D. Brown
and Sons Limited, Bridgend, 1995

British Library Cataloguing in Publication Data.
A catalogue record for this book is available from the
British Library.

ISBN 0-7083-1285-3

The Publishers wish to acknowledge the financial
assistance of the Arts Council of Wales towards the cost
of producing this volume.